FREE TO
BELIEVE

FREE TO BELIEVE

◆

DAVID JENKINS
BISHOP OF DURHAM
& REBECCA JENKINS

BBC BOOKS

Also by David Jenkins, Bishop of Durham:

Guide to the Debate about God
The Glory of Man
Still Living with Questions
The Contradiction of Christianity
God, Miracle and the Church of England
God, the Future and Politics
God, Jesus and Life in the Spirit

The authors are grateful to Professor K. Thompson of the Faculty of Social Sciences, the Open University, for an interim report of his study of the letters sent to the Bishop of Durham, 1984–6. The material on pages 23–5 is based on this report.

Published by BBC Books,
a division of BBC Enterprises Limited,
Woodlands, 80 Wood Lane, London W12 0TT
First published 1991
© The Right Reverend D. E. Jenkins and Rebecca Jenkins 1991

ISBN 0 563 20914 3 (paperback)
ISBN 0 563 36240 5 (hardback)

Set in 11/13pt Bembo by Ace Filmsetting Ltd, Frome, Somerset
Printed and bound in Great Britain by Redwood Press, Melksham, Wiltshire
Cover printed by Clays Ltd, St Ives plc

Contents

Preface

How can a book presented in the first person be written by two persons? The answer in this case arises out of an unusual family collaboration. The text is written in the person of David Jenkins, Bishop of Durham. The structure and composition is, however, the work of his daughter, Rebecca Jenkins. The reason they both feel this is a valid form of composition lies in their particular working relationship. For the last six years Rebecca Jenkins has worked as the Bishop of Durham's Research Assistant and Press Officer. As such she has been closely involved with David Jenkins in answering the immense correspondence which has developed, transcribing and editing his speeches, keeping archives of interviews and papers, acting as go-between and agent in all his relations with the media. It is this experience – and the sympathy of mind grown out of the affection of a lifetime – which has enabled her to write this book by ordering and weaving together either what the Bishop of Durham has specifically written, or the content of his thought and argument, distilled and put into other words. The outline of this book, the arguments of each chapter and the draft of every page have been discussed again and again between the two authors.

The resulting book presents and represents David Jenkins's thoughts. So it is correctly written with himself as first person, but it must be clearly acknowledged and stated that the pain, care and setting of the actual composition is throughout that of Rebecca Jenkins. This is why we both sign this Preface and why our names are necessarily and equally on the title page.

David Jenkins
Rebecca Jenkins
Auckland Castle.

1

Where I Start From

———————◆———————

In February 1984 an announcement from Downing Street transformed one Professor David Jenkins of Leeds University into David Dunelm, Bishop of Durham in the Church of England. During the months that followed a man who had spent his life as a fairly orthodox Anglican theologian saw his public character suffer a sea-change in the eye of a media storm. 'Blasphemer', ran the headlines, 'doubting bishop', even 'antichrist', and always – but always – 'the controversial Bishop of Durham'.

As I am now well over half way through my episcopate (should the Lord spare me, and perhaps, afflict others until I reach retirement age) it has been pressed upon me that the time has come for a review of the last six years and some public self-explanation. Hence this book. I hope that readers may find something of interest in this personal story of 'the doubting bishop' who was – and is – actually and honestly a believing bishop.

The first outing of the media caricature of the Doubting Bishop came as a result of an interview broadcast in April 1984. *Credo* was a religious television programme which followed a well-tried format. Guests came to the *Credo* studio to engage with an interviewer in serious and thoughtful discussion on topics of faith. Informative Sunday afternoon viewing for those interested in religion but not, one might have thought, a likely source of public controversy. Early in 1984 the producers were looking about for a mainstream Anglican theologian to explain the present state of biblical scholarship and how Christians believed today. Lambeth Palace was approached for advice and suggested the then Professor of Theology at Leeds. So it was that I found myself, one cold day in early spring, in a London television studio arguing for the traditional and orthodox Christian belief that Jesus was, in a real sense, both God and Man. In the course of the discussion I made some brief remarks about the interpretation of the Resurrection stories, the symbolic and mythological nature of the story of the Virgin Birth and the existence of miracle stories in all religious traditions. As I understood it, I was merely trying to clear unnecessary obstacles out of the way in order to get on to discussing the real issues of living in faith today. All the points I made were in the mainstream of Christian theological discussion and had been so for over seventy years. I climbed back into my train for the journey home, weary but with a sense of duty done; I certainly had no inkling that in this recording I had laid a theological mine.

The *Credo* interview was finally broadcast on 29 April 1984. In the intervening weeks the Leeds professor had been announced as the new Bishop of Durham and, with the able assistance of the press, the 'Durham Affair' began. 'Doubting Bishop – Jesus not Born of a Virgin.' 'Bishop's Theology Questioned' (and, some pages later, 'Durham Clergy Stand By Bishop Designate', but that was hardly news). By June there were '11 Clergy in Call to Put Off Consecration' and a petition was delivered to the Archbishop of York with 12 500 signatures – according to one report – requesting that the Bishop Elect should not be consecrated. The Archbishop stood firm and on 6 July the consecration service took place in the splendid Minster at York. The General Synod of the Church of England was then gathering for its summer meeting in the city, so an unusually high number of bishops took part in the service. Despite two brief protests, the service was a very moving occasion for me and I shall always remember the warmth and support of that congregation.

In the early hours of a hot summer night three days later, fire broke out in the roof of the Minster destroying much of the South Transept. From that moment on, the Bishop of Durham was news whether he liked it or not. The vivid images of the burning cathedral caught both media and public imagination and toured the world. I have press cuttings from the USA, Australia, New Zealand, India, Africa, Japan and the Gulf States, some sent by friends, some by protesters. The view that this fire had been an Act of God, a sign of His displeasure at the consecration of an unsuitable bishop, gave the media a lively angle and struck a chord in the public consciousness. At least the headline writers enjoyed themselves. 'That Thunderbolt Was No Coincidence.' 'Was the Fire a Message From God?' How far those who held that the Almighty had decided to intervene with a thunderbolt considered the implications of their position was not clear. Was the Lord so inefficient as to miss the object of His wrath by several days? (Or, as one rival theory went, was He really aiming at General Synod which was to meet the next day?) Are we to suppose God to be so petty and limited that all He could think of to do was to set fire to a cathedral? The whole affair brought out how strongly a 'primitive' belief in an arbitrary and vengeful God who exercises supernatural (in the sense of magical) powers is alive, if not entirely healthy.

A sadder side of the media-stimulated reaction was the evidence of how much the area of religious belief and practice is for many people charged with intense anxiety and sometimes fear. This was made apparent in the amount of 'hate mail', sent to both the Archbishop of York and myself, which the combination of fire, lightning and controversy over belief or unbelief, stirred up. Many of the letters were not without their comical side. A family favourite was one which ran to several pages of abuse but ended simply with, 'may you rot in hell', signed 'a true Christian'. On the other hand, the hell of uncontrolled fear and hatred in which some of these writers appeared to be living gave rise to serious questions about what religion meant in their lives. From the beginning each bout of intense media coverage produced between 1000 and 2000 letters on top of normal 'business' correspondence. Even at the very height of the most hostile press coverage the ratio never fell below three letters of support to every two letters of protest. Given that, according to sociologists and psychologists, people are much more inclined to write to protest than to support, I cannot help but believe that

I was never alone, however 'controversial' I was held to be by some.

In September 1984 I came to preach my first sermon as a bishop in the Cathedral at Durham. The occasion was the Enthronement service, an ancient ceremony held to mark the formal accession of the new incumbent to the See. I was coming to a diocese with a strong mining tradition at a time when the County of Durham was deeply moved by a major national miners' strike. It seemed to me that if a Christian leader was to talk about God and hope (the subject of my sermon was 'The Cost of Hope') then he had to show what he meant in real terms. The reality that was gripping the Durham community at that time was the miners' strike. Therefore the first two-thirds of my text were about the resources that God shows us for the support of hope in even the most difficult times. In the last part of the sermon I tried to relate the general message to the existing situation. My theme was that if both sides in the conflict would see that there was wrongness in some parts of their position, then they could be brought to compromise and to the resolution of a terrible struggle which was causing much misery. At the York consecration service that summer an old friend of mine in preaching his sermon said that bishops, generally speaking, are generally speaking. I resolved when I first became a bishop that I would continue the habit of a lifetime and risk bringing my theology down to reality. In taking the risk of coming down to earth there is always the danger of making wrong judgements. As there is only one God, and ultimately all we humans can do is trust in the one God, I continue to believe that such risks must be faced. In reports of this Enthronement sermon the media picked up a new tone. No longer was this bishop merely 'doubting', he was now a 'turbulent priest' interfering in politics as well. These two media labels have persisted ever since. From my own point of view, the *Credo* interview and my Enthronement sermon set out the theological lines I have been pursuing all my life and will continue to pursue as long as I am able. The one concerns the way we are to understand the Biblical texts and how that reflects our understanding of God and how He works in our world. The other is to do with how we Christians should understand the commandmant to love our neighbours in our everyday lives and communities. These two strands link together under two fundamental convictions: that a real faith in the one true God enables us to face reality at all times; and that no one can be fully human until we are all enabled to be fully human.

'The turbulent priest' and the 'Doubting Bishop of Durham' were creations of the media headline writers of 1984. The man behind the headlines had spent sixty years becoming himself. As my story is one of a personal pilgrimage made public, perhaps I should fill in a little biographical background. I was born in South London in 1925. My father was an insurance inspector in the City and my brother and I grew up in a comfortable, caring home. I long held the impression that my Grandfather Jenkins was born in Wales, but when sorting out my father's papers after his recent death at the grand age of ninety-six, my brother discovered some family birth certificates which revealed that my grandfather was born in Wiltshire. Any Welsh roots I have go back to a great-grandfather who was born in Cardiff – though the family's Celtic tinge was strengthened by a grand-mother who came from Helston in Cornwall.

My parents were regular attenders at the local Methodist church. There was a strong Wesleyan tradition in the family; both my grandfathers were active lay preachers and travelled the circuit. I can remember seeing one of my grandfathers, Mr Page, in the pulpit. I do not recall much by the way of conversa-tion with him, but I remember his caring and his interest. He seemed to me an immensely kindly and powerful man in a quiet way – he was not particularly vibrant or emphatic. My picture of him is of a benevolent, white-haired gentleman with a mous-tache. He was a master carpenter. I was his first grandchild, and his first male descendant – his two children had both been daughters – and I am told he doted on me. He certainly left me with a very affectionate memory of him. Grandfather Page died when I was about seven years old but his influence left an imprint on me. Much later, after my ordination as a priest, I came back to preach at Bromley Methodist Church and a very old man told my mother that I sounded exactly like Mr Page.

My parents first put me into a Sunday school at the age of eight. I must have been a rather horrid and bumptious child, for my clearest memory of this is getting quite annoyed at being treated as if I were only eight. This Sunday school was led by a dear lady who was really very nice and quite entertaining but I felt that she never explained the reasons for what she taught. From as early as I can recall I was always interested, not in what people said, but why they said it and what it meant. This questioning habit led me on a quest which brought me eventually to a Crusader class – a boys' Bible class – which happened to be attached to an evangelical Church of England church called Christ Church in Bromley. It was a big class, run by a very lively collection of men. We gathered for Sunday afternoon meetings where we sang with vigour and were addressed with vigour. We were encouraged to rummage in the Bible and studied it verse by verse. We discovered things like, God is interested in us and that is what Jesus is about. It was in this class that I became convinced that God was interested in me and that I ought to follow up this something I had found. Sometime around the age of eleven I made a commitment inside myelf. I decided that this is for me, and whatever 'it' is I am going to join up. (The technical phrase for this is 'born again' but, as is evident to lots of people now, the 'new birth' did not entirely take with me, so I am careful about using the phrase.)

This feeling of call and of being caught up in something exciting was reinforced one summer when I went on a harvest camp in Buckinghamshire. The corn dust had an unfortunate effect on my hay fever and I was laid aside with an asthmatic attack. A local curate befriended me. He was what is termed 'high church' and through him I became interested in taking part in services as a server and discovered the beauty of the Anglican liturgy. Somehow the shape and music of the Anglican services fitted in well with my perceptions of life, adding a sense of mystery and a deepening sense of worship which built in me an intense feeling of the universal importance of the love of God, a love which I felt increasingly caught up by. Although my way into the Faith was through Jesus, I was from the very beginning led through Jesus beyond the formal horizons of the church to the importance of God and His purposes in the whole world. Encounters with evangelists through the Bible class I attended emphasised this world view. I was particularly struck by the message and approach of an evangelist from the Children's Special Service Mission – a body which specialised in children's services at seaside resorts and held holiday camps for young people. Another time I met a doctor who had been a missionary. We talked about mission and why he did it. I decided I too was caught up by the call to pass on all this excitement I experienced. By the time I was twelve I formed an idea that I might want to be a missionary – even, at one point, a missionary bishop. But this was probably connected with the fact that I had just started at St Dunstan's School in Catford (St Dunstan was a bishop of some note).

I enjoyed school. I was not much of a sportsman but I had a natural liking for reading. I was fond of any book on history – an interest which did not always find favour with my vicar. I remember the disgust of this gentleman when he discovered me reading some nineteenth-century rationalist work which insisted on treating Jesus as nothing more than a man and attempted to explain away miracles. I did not swallow the thesis of such books whole, but they did make me aware that there were all sorts of questions around. The writings of Bishop Gore became a favourite, particularly his three books on 'the Reconstruction of Belief'. Bishop Gore was an Anglo-Catholic who was an academic in Oxford from 1875 and eventually became a notable Anglican bishop, first of Birmingham then Oxford. In 1889 he edited some essays under the title 'Lux Mundi' (Light of the World) which upset many of the older high church theologians because they were addressed to critical questions about the Bible and about Christian tradition. Bishop Gore's writings put me onto the possibility of attempts to reconcile critical use of the Bible with orthodox faith. Somehow it never seemed odd to me to pick up information on the background and history of the Bible. The Bible was the story of people discovering God in history and talking about discovering God in their times. It unfolded as a very human and historical work as well as being a profoundly religious and exciting book.

The Second World War broke out while I was at St Dunstan's School and at the age of eighteen I was called up in the routine way. I became a cadet for the Royal Artillery, was commissioned round about the time of VE Day and sent out to India. I was very lucky. I went into the army at a stage when the war in Europe was well on its way and I never had to fight. I enjoyed my time in the army and even wondered briefly whether I might want to be a professional army officer. I think I found the camaraderie of army life attractive and, of course, the first experience of foreign lands is always exciting.

One of the main lessons I learnt in the army was of the balance between interdependence and leadership. An episode that remains in my mind was of an occasion when I found myself in charge of returning a convoy of ammunition (which mercifully we no longer needed as the war was over) to the ordnance depot at Jabalpur. I will never forget the moment of realisation that of all the personnel depending on me in some eighty lorries loaded with ammunition, I was the only English-speaking person about. I did my best with what I had learnt of Urdu and with a lot of goodwill we somehow got the ammunition to its destination. It was a vivid illustration of how dependent the 'man in charge' is on the rest of the team.

India had a great effect on me. It was an experience of a very different culture which opened me out into an appreciation of just how broad, mysterious and exciting the world is. It was my first introduction to a multi-faith society. Fascinating conversations with Muslims, Hindus and Parsees enriched the sense of the splendid diversity of things. On the other hand, some aspects of the sub-continent presented a challenge to belief in a loving God. I particularly remember travelling through a cholera-stricken area where men, women and children lay dying by the roadside. Yet overall impressions reinforced the feeling of excitement and worship. The magnificent countryside gave vivid expression to this – moments such as travelling up a road leading to Tibet, rounding a corner and suddenly seeing the Himalayas. The Te Deum, the ancient hymn of praise to God, seemed the only natural response. 'We praise Thee, O God, we acknowledge Thee to be the Lord.'

My love affair with the Indian countryside was crystallised for me in a trip I took into the mountains. Being young and not thinking, perhaps, of my mother as much as I should, I took the chance of a month's leave to travel up into the Himalayas rather than go home. I travelled with a friend of mine who later was to become my brother-in-law – though at the time I had not yet met his sister. We hired, in the approved style, some Sherpa porters and a Gurkha cook and set out for the borders of Tibet with Rudyard Kipling firmly in mind. One day we were toiling up a sharp mountain face which led out of the lowlands into the heights. My friend, ahead of me, disturbed a large, grey animal which I imagined to be a langur-type monkey. It was only after our return, on reading up on the subject, that I discovered that we had been too high up for langur monkeys. We had, in fact, been in the Teesta Valley which, in its higher reaches, is one of the places where yetis have been sighted. I have therefore taken the line that, although I did not know it at the time, I spotted a yeti. It is my story, and I am sticking to it. I stumbled upon what others have searched for for years. The truth, of course, remains a mystery. The story comes in useful when talking to schoolchildren.

I left India in 1947 with a strong feeling that cut and dried answers can only deal with a restricted part of the world. Our preconceptions must always be challenged by wider experiences. Alongside this, meetings and conversations with Indian Christians sharpened a sense of the particularity and depth of faith. Each person may not believe in the same way but belief continues because people are caught up in the stories of faith and in continuing worship – a reality which reflects the independent source of faith and its independence, in particular, from culture.

I returned to England to take up a place at Queen's College, Oxford, where I embarked upon a classical degree followed by a Theology degree. I read Greats first – Greek and Latin languages and literature, Philosophy and Ancient History – partly because of my attraction to working things out. I was clear that you must serve God with your mind as well as with your heart and soul. Part of the attraction of Ancient History was that it concerned the world into which Christ came. Instinctively I was convinced that you needed to understand the context as well as the message.

Many people say that the experience of university changed their pattern of belief. I was not conscious that my beliefs changed at Oxford, rather that they grew and developed. One of the main shifts of emphasis that emerged in that period of my life was that I found my faith becoming more and more God-centred. Of course, Jesus was always about God anyway, but the God-centredness symbolised more for me the way God spreads out to take in everything. In this way I found that it is by being drawn deeper and deeper into the mysticism of Faith that you find the ability to take on more and more of the complexities of the world.

While at Oxford I married the sister of my friend and in 1952 we moved to Birmingham where I was ordained deacon to serve in the Cathedral in the centre of the city. I was priested a year later. I have two clear memories of my ordination. The first was waking up the Monday after being made a priest and thinking to myself with rather a shock: right, nothing to look forward to now. This is what I have been aiming at; now I have simply got to be a priest. The second was walking back with my mother from preaching my first sermon as a priest. She looked rather abstracted and finally confessed that she had not been attending to what I had said in my sermon because she was so reminded of how, when I was quite small, I used to line up the chairs and preach to them. The influence of Grandfather Page, I suppose. I have always found the family a useful guard against taking oneself too seriously.

At Birmingham I became involved in lecturing at Queen's Theological College. There happened to be a vacancy for someone to do doctrine and I was asked to fill in. So from the very beginning of my working life I embarked on a pattern I think I have followed ever since, that is a combination of pastoral and worship work on the one hand and academic work concerned with thinking things out on the other. This fascination with thinking things through, working them out, wrestling them out, has been a major thread throughout my life. From Birmingham we returned to Oxford, now with two sons, and I became chaplain at my old College, Queen's. After fifteen years and the birth of two daughters we decided to up sticks and move to Geneva where I had been offered a job with the World Council of Churches.

At the WCC I was given the imposing title of 'Director of Humanum Studies' – a brief sufficiently broad to allow me to explore a wide range of international questions with people of other churches and other cultures. The job took me round the world in pursuit of issues such as race, health care and the relation of faith to social questions. Colleagues from other countries presented vivid and real challenges to home-grown assumptions. Challenges such as, if people are oppressed, exploited and life means nothing to them, how are they to get the message of the Gospel? It became clearer and clearer that if, after all, Jesus is the Son of the God of the whole world – the whole universe – then any of the questions which trouble the human race must be substance and subject for Christians to wrestle with.

My experience with the WCC had a profound effect in making me forever (until the End!) a displaced person. That is to say, I could no longer be sure that where I belonged (such as being British) was enough. This displacement seemed to be part of entering into the fullness of the purposes of God, part of helping to fight the things that are against the purposes of God and – as far as we are concerned in this life – is probably endless.

It was from the basis of my Geneva experiences and encounters that I wrote a book called *The Contradiction of Christianity*, published in 1976. In this I set out the thesis that the Marxist analysis which has shaped so many political systems in our world, raises many important questions and presents challenges which Christianity must face. The argument being that, although I believe that the conclusions Marxists come to are wrong, much of the analysis is useful and Christian faith not only must, but is quite able to, face this fact.

In 1973 our family returned to the United Kingdom, this time to Manchester, where I had been appointed Director of the William Temple Foundation. Archbishop William Temple was the great socially concerned Archbishop of Canterbury whose immense sense of the universality of God (and what he called the 'materiality' of the Christian faith) led him into 'controversy' in his day as he felt compelled to bring the Gospel into social problems, focusing on the interaction between faith and society. The connection with Archbishop Temple was important to me as he is perhaps the nearest thing I have to a hero. The Foundation in Manchester named after him was concerned with looking at the effects and structures of institutions, on the principle that the Church is finding its way in the modern world and as part of this theology and faith needs to understand structures. The members of the William Temple Foundation work with 'concerned operatives', whether in hospitals, industry or the inner city, clarifying the effects of the institutions that surround them. ('Concerned operatives' are people who, while getting on with their jobs, consider questions about whether it is the right job, and how it might be changed and improved.)

The work of the WTF picked up an interest of mine which goes back a long way in my life. While a chaplain at Queen's College, Oxford, I had been involved in groups looking at linguistic structures and the structures of institutions (in the area of doctor/patient relationships asking, say, what it means to wear a white coat and other such mundane but actually quite important questions). My years in Manchester were very valuable in expanding my direct experience of industrial and social issues. Despite the grand-sounding title of 'Foundation', the reality was four or five members of a team who took practical part in real situations. One project involved members of the Foundation with the Ebbw Vale community while it struggled to come to terms with the closing down of the steelworks there. In various situations and all around the country the WTF worked – and still works – with other groups in developing practical theology in everyday life.

I left the William Temple Foundation to move to be professor of Theology and Religious Studies at Leeds University in 1979. This was the first time I had returned to a purely academic post since my Oxford days and I imagined at the time that it would be my last job. A gentle, though interesting, end to a varied career. Then, in 1983, the Bishop of Durham moved to become Archbishop of York and the See became vacant. When the first hint came that I was being considered for the appointment, my initial reaction was not immediately joyful. I was nearly sixty, my life had been spent freelancing on the frontiers and I imagined that this was where my contribution to mission had come. But my wife said: 'You have been preaching for years about being ready to go on journeys and taking risks. You can't just settle down now merely because you are nearly sixty.' So together we decided I should accept. It was also conveyed to me, in that particularly subtle way of the Church of England, that certain people, whom I respect, wanted me to take the job. In the end I realised that it would be a betrayal of what the Church of England has meant to me if I refused to respond to the challenge.

The acceptance of this challenge and the appointment meant sometimes bewildering changes for the family. The exchange of an average semi-detached house in the suburbs of Leeds for the historic splendours of Auckland Castle, for one. The official residence in Bishop Auckland, a small market town some twelve miles down the road from Durham City, has been a country home of the Bishops of Durham from the thirteenth century onwards. It started life as a manor house and hunting lodge of the Prince Bishop and eventually became the principal residence when Bishop Van Mildert gave the castle in Durham over to found the university in the early nineteenth century. It is a large and rambling place which now houses diocesan offices as well as two flats, and some staterooms around a core of rooms which are the bishop's home. There are considerable pressures to 'living on the job', particularly in an ancient monument but – due in large part to the great skills of my wife, without whom I would not survive – it is a house with a very friendly atmosphere, despite its size.

There are obviously problems with the concept of a Christian leader living in such grandeur. I decided that as I was rising sixty when I came to this job, I could only take on the conditions of it and work from that basis. The compromise vividly illustrates the fundamental fact that if you are trying to draw the attention of society at large, or groups in society, to poverty on one hand, or the wickedness of society on the other, no one speaks from a position of sinlessness. I have always thought that the whole business of Christian faith and of being human is what I would call solidarity in sin. You are compromised all the time. The question is, what compromises do you take on in the knowledge that it is only with the Grace of God that you can make something of them? No Christian preaches the Gospel on the basis of being a good advertisement for it, but only on the basis of being totally dependent on the love and power of God to take him or her forward.

Grandeur aside, however, it is a great privilege to live in such a lovely location. I take great pleasure in walking and watching the marvellous variations of nature and Auckland Castle provides plenty of opportunity for such pleasures. There is a large bowling green just outside the front door to walk around and watch the seasons change. With a quarter of an hour to spare you can walk into the park where a stream winds through on its way to the River Wear. There is always a chance of spotting a kingfisher or maybe a dipper, a hawk or kestrel. On a neighbouring farmer's land there is a well-established heronry whose occupants often fly over. There are rabbits everywhere, the occasional hare, an odd weasel and sometimes a deer or two who wander over open land from nearby estates. One of the past bishops was a tree collector of some note and although many of his expensive imports have now disappeared through neglect, traces of his passion for beautiful trees persist. When autumn comes there is a whole little valley running up the park where a collection of trees display a magnificent mixture of umber and scarlet.

No two Bishops of Durham have been much alike in style. Though there is some dispute (depending on where you start counting) as to the precise number, I became something like the sixty-ninth Bishop of Durham. The portraits of many of my predecessors hang in the staterooms which take up a large section of the castle. On canvas the majority of them do not look a particularly inspiring bunch; however, in history they stand as an interesting collection of men. Cardinal Wolsey was one, although he never actually managed to make a visit to his See. It seems he intended to come as he had a special kind of bulrush planted in a pond in the grounds to provide the type of scented floorcovering he favoured. However, death intervened in his plans. There is a story that a butler at the castle in the first part of this century came upon his ghost in the oratory, which might indicate that he regretted this fact.

There is a tradition of scholarly incumbents of the See and of these I find Bishop Joseph Barber Lightfoot (1879–89) interesting. He was a man of great learning who made considerable contributions to studies of the New Testament and the Apostolic Fathers. The practical side of his nature was deeply concerned that there should be appropriate Church buildings and Church institutions in the cities and towns that were spreading across the area following the industrialisation of the Victorian period. He founded several churches and such things as the Lightfoot Institute in Bishop Auckland which provided a library and educational facilities to the community. Particularly interested in the proper theological training of the clergy, he had groups of candidates to live with him in Auckland Castle while they trained. The archives contain photographs of him with these, his 'lambs', solemn young men in stiff black suits. In Bishop Lightfoot there was a combination of scholarship, concern for ministry, and a concern for the accessibility of the Church on the ground in the communities, which seems very important to me.

Lightfoot's successor was Bishop Brooke Foss Wescott (1889–1901). His is one of the best portraits in the Throne Room – a marvellous Victorian face, full of character and determination. He was involved more than once in mediation during miners' disputes in the Durham coalfields. According to one story he once summoned both the union leaders and management to Bishop Auckland and shut them into the library, refusing to let them out until they came to an agreement.

Before the Second World War the See was held by Bishop Hensley Henson (1920–39). Bishop Henson had a powerful capacity to make points, sometimes in a witty way and sometimes in a cutting way. His speeches in the House of Lords and elsewhere got him into trouble because he was rather good at following up an argument with a certain amount of forcefulness. He had his own way of looking at things and thinking about things, and was determined to follow his thoughts in a responsible manner. I have some fellow feeling with him because he suffered a fuss over his first appointment as Bishop (to the Diocese of Hereford) when some people objected to his approach to the New Testament and the Creed. Reading about this controversy gives one a certain feeling of *déjà vu*. Sixty or seventy years later, sections of the Church are still reluctant to face questions raised at the time of Bishop Henson's appointment.

One of my predecessors was a special friend. I first met Ian Ramsey (Bishop of Durham from 1966 to 1972) while I was a chaplain at Queen's College, Oxford, and worked with him on several things to do with the relationship between faith and institutions. He was the person who first showed me round Auckland Castle. He took great pride in the beautiful chapel, which was restored under his successor Bishop (and now Archbishop of York) John Habgood. He is now buried there. He died in the job and is much missed. He was a great colleague whose commitment to living at the interface between faith and practice, and philosophy, faith and theology, had a great influence on me. It has been very moving to find myself one of his successors.

Auckland Castle contains many reminders of the Bishopric's more recent incumbents but to get a real sense of the origins of Christianity in the North East you need to make a trip to the Cathedral Church in Durham. In this magnificent Norman building where the tombs of St Cuthbert and his chronicler, the Venerable Bede, lie under soaring arches of sandstone, there is a real sense that in the middle of all the changes and chances of this fleeting world there is an amazing continuity of the knowledge of God, of faith in God, of the worship of God. Every time I go into the cathedral I feel I am in the middle of something really lasting. This has its awesome side. When I was first shown round the cathedral as a new bishop I heard a mason chipping. My guide and I rounded a pillar and found the man working on a large stone panel bearing a list of names. He was adding my name at the foot of the list of bishops. As I looked at my name inscribed on that ancient wall I thought – this is so absurd I can only rely on God. When it comes to relying on God any Bishop of Durham has an excellent example in our most illustrious predecessor, St Cuthbert, the father of Northumbrian spirituality, whose story takes place in the earliest Christian times of our island.

The island of Lindisfarne, or Holy Island, stands off the Northumbrian coast, separated from the mainland by a tidal causeway where sea-birds feed from the rich mud left by the receding waves. Monks first came to Lindisfarne in 635 with St Aidan, who left his monastery at Iona to set up a sister house under the patronage of Oswald, King of Northumbria. According to Bede, St Cuthbert left his secular life to become a monk in response to a vision telling him of the death of Aidan. He followed that saint to Holy Island where his diligence and piety led his brother monks to select him to become a hermit on the neighbouring island of Inner Farne. The surrounding islands, rocky and inhospitable, were believed in those days to be inhabited by demons and only the holiest of monks were considered strong enough to do battle with them. In these island demons of loneliness and of nature's arbitrary power, the hermits of the seventh century confronted both the depths of evil and uncertainty within themselves and the dangers and unpredictability of the earthly universe around them. Through the rigours of this harsh existence St Cuthbert kept a very direct sense of God. Cut off from the outside world by dangerous seas, he chose the very remotest part of his island as the site of his hermitage. There he dug a cell with walls but no roof so that all he could see was the sky. It was a kind of focusing, a containing of horizons so as to put himself at the centre of a burning glass where he and God could come closer and closer together.

The aim of Cuthbert's life was, in one way, to cut himself off from the world altogether. Yet, when he was finally persuaded, with great reluctance, to leave his hermitage and become a bishop, his concentration on God gave him great freedom for his neighbours. He was prepared to go anywhere to preach the

Gospel to people, and was never put off by the wildness and inaccessibility of many of the parts of Northumbria in those times. The asceticism of St Cuthbert is too costly for our times but the concentration of mind and readiness to cast off all sorts of things symbolised in his life, point to something not irrelevant to our present. Today, when we have very nearly been swept away by the notion that life consists of the number of things you can consume, the demanding element in Cuthbert – the giving up in order to get onto that which is really worthwhile – is something that needs to be steadily, soberly and fairly cheerfully built back into life.

I have a particular affection for St Cuthbert and his Holy Island of Lindisfarne. According to the stories of Bede, which are our principal record of the saint's life, he had an openness to people which grew out of his sheer desire to share. This seemed to be part of something he had spotted about God which also extended to his being open to the wonders and glories of nature. Cuthbert seems to have had a way with animals which I find very endearing. In one story the saint spends the night praying standing up to his neck in the sea. As dawn breaks he comes out to be greeted, in the words of Bede, by 'two four-footed creatures that are commonly called otters. These, prostrate before him on the sand, began to warm his feet with their breath and sought to dry him with their fur. When they had finished their ministrations they received his blessing and slipped away into their native waters.' In another vignette, Cuthbert remonstrates with two ravens who are picking pieces from the shelter he has built on Inner Farne. The birds are so stricken by his words they bring him some pig fat as a peace offering, which visiting monks then use to grease their boots. (For all their sense of the miraculous, medieval story-tellers still kept a marvellous sense of earthly priorities.) Despite the gloss of exaggerated holiness and miraculousness of these stories – a style typical of the records of saints – the theme of Cuthbert's affinity to nature and animals carries certain chords of truth for me. I have had a badger walk up to me in broad daylight on the South Downs at a time when I felt absolutely quiet and at one with my surroundings (at such moments, I hope, I am at one with God). When you are on the

God wavelength you are also on the natural wavelength, so I am not at all surprised that St Cuthbert and the animals got on well together.

There is something about Lindisfarne that focuses for me the sense that God has to do directly with me and I have to do with God. The island is special to me for many reasons – its peace, the birdwatching I can do there, the sense of openness in the wind under its wide skies – but also for an incident that happened to me there on my first visit several years ago. I had come up for a day from the friary at Alnmouth where I was staying in order to have some quiet. I was trying to think out certain questions that were circulating in my mind about the relationship between God and the world, miracles and Jesus. I was making all sorts of notes but my thoughts were not coming together properly for the book I was trying to write. I wandered all around the island, listening to the eider ducks muttering to themselves. Not exactly praying but contemplating. I was coming back towards the road when I suddenly saw a skylark singing on the ground which reminded me of the Te Deum. It made me think that there is something in everything which is singing and glorious and I am onto it. As I returned to the road, at the bottom where the pavement began, I saw a perfectly clean playing card lying face down on the tarmac. I knew before I went over to it what sort of card it would be. I picked it up and turned it over – it was the joker. I still have it. I thought, something is going to happen and I bet God is playing a joke on me.

I was asked to be Bishop of Durham soon after that. My playing card remains a vivid personal connection with Holy Island for me – it is almost as if St Cuthbert dealt me the joker. It said to me, you are mixed up in things you do not know about, which are far more than you can understand; the best you can do is to be ready to get on with it. I have tried to be ready to get on with it ever since, even when at times my personal pilgrimage becomes uncomfortably public. Sometimes I wonder, is it the joker or is it God – or are they one and the same?

2

'An Unbelieving Bishop'

◆

At the heart of the self who questions, I am a simple believer. I believe God is, and He is as He is in Jesus. It is clear to me that there is something and someone at the heart of things who cares for, and works for, holiness, the blazing beauty of love, justice and peace. I am also clear that as a Christian teacher and believer I am called to explain as specifically and practically as I can what difference Christian believing, worshipping and practising makes today and to life at large. To learn the meaning of faith by exploring the questions of faith, with the help of the gifts of faith, is simply living out what it means to believe in God.

How then did the pursuit of such belief lead to charges of faithlessness? One factor was the extraordinary way in which many people seem to believe newspaper headlines or short newspaper reports. To have personal experience of how reports can start by being misleading and end up by being quite untrue, combined with personal knowledge of indignant and distressed accusations based on such grossly simplified and untrue reports, is to be reminded just how credulous and uncritical people can be. What struck me as being of wider concern was that public reactions often seemed to indicate a trivialising of truth, not just in certain sections of the media, but also in public responses to media reports. We seem at present to suffer from a climate of opinion in which what you might call 'extended conversational thinking' is neglected. That is extended conversational thinking as a process which involves controversy and conflict as a normal way of investigating worthwhile things, as a reasonable form of politics, and as the only sensible way of tackling the complexities of the world and the different perspectives people have. Its neglect in favour of sharpening all issues into slogans can only impoverish democracy and prevent creative, open debate.

I made a conscious decision when I was called to be a bishop that I would go on being David Jenkins, the Christian disciple; David Jenkins who knew whatever he knew about the New Testament; David Jenkins who would explain how the Faith and what he knew fitted together; David Jenkins who was concerned to pursue what it meant to respond to God. It seemed to me important that my personal commitment and discipleship should not be distorted by having this rather unusual role of bishop. However, public reaction portrayed in the media seemed to indicate that many people felt that once a believer becomes a bishop the demands of personal discipleship should be wholly submitted to the demands of the 'representative' nature of the new role.

The role was assumed to have suppressed the person, and the task of the role was assumed to have suppressed the duty to think for oneself, and as oneself. For example, a common objection was that what could be said by a theologian was not appropriate for public statement by a bishop. As one journalist put it to me, surely a bishop was a kind of 'pastoral politician' and must realise that he is not just talking for himself and his own personal vision of Christianity but that he is talking for the authority of the Church and for a wide range of opinions in the Church. This view – which opposes 'personal' responsibility to 'traditional' responsibility – seems to me to strike at the very heart of truth and of the responsibility of the individual believer within the Tradition for passing on the living truth of the Tradition. It is plainly unreasonable, plainly faithless and plainly impracticable. It is plainly unreasonable because if a question is there it must be faced. 'The Tradition' cannot decide what are real questions (the Tradition could not shut up a Galileo or Darwin, for example). But in any case the attitude is faithless because if we really believe in God then we can face any real challenge. It is also impracticable because the faithful cannot hide from real questions forever. Real questions will keep coming up. Furthermore, the glory and saving love of God is to be shared well beyond the boundaries of 'us' believers. We cannot begin by asking people to believe three impossible things before breakfast. What needs to be presented is engagement with the living God who is at work in every aspect of life anywhere in the universe.

I must admit that I was surprised and disturbed by the evidence of an absence of a concern for truth among some self-styled defenders of Christian faith and orthodoxy. Among most of the articles and many of the letters I read at the time of the first controversies there was hardly any discussion of whether the views I expressed were valid, or could reasonably be held to be valid. The arguments almost entirely centred around whether I, as a bishop, was entitled to pursue publicly those theological questions I pursued as a professor. The argument that the pursuit of truth is to be suppressed or ignored in the interests of a responsibility to God and His Church surely borders on the blasphemous. Can we really accept that a mere shift of institutional responsibility represented by moving from the job of university teacher to that of a bishop, can justify two different and incompatible sets of criteria for truth?

Take, for instance, the matter of the interpretation of the biblical texts. The questions raised by critical biblical scholarship are not the ravings of a few marginal radicals; the scholarship is sound and has been well established now for something like a century or so. Simple inspection of the biblical records shows that they do not fit together in literal details; they work together as various and varied expressions of faith experienced. To deny that there are inconsistencies in the Gospels, and demand a literalist or fundamentalist approach to them, is a little like expecting science to ignore the work of Einstein or Newton, or of Harvey in the circulation of the blood. Rational thought cannot deny what has been discovered.

At the level of practising faith it does not matter who says what as to which bits of the Bible you should believe, or precisely how the biblical texts get you onto the historical Jesus. On these matters the debate will go on from generation to generation as it has always done. But no one can expect to find a clear and absolute authority in the texts. The crux of the matter is that a desire for absolute authority is faithless. If God cannot cope with the things that have subsequently happened to His world – such as the discoveries of science or of critical, historical scholarship – then He cannot be the Creator, let alone the Redeemer.

The media fuss of 1984 and 1985 revealed that previous theological discussions – such as that prompted by the appointment of Bishop Hensley Henson in the late 1920s – had been confined to a relatively select group. In the 1980s, television programmes such as *Credo* and *The Gnostics* began to put many of the issues together and raise them to wider public attention. Thus the churches' collective bluff was called. It became publicly apparent that the institutional Church was not facing many of the issues posed by the developments of modern science, by advances in the critical study of the Bible, and in historical analysis – developments that had been emerging since the seventeenth century. The Bishop of Durham might have been responsible for triggering an explosion but the explosive material had been collecting for a long time. I believe that practically everybody at my level of the Church knows perfectly well that these questions have to be faced. However, some of them believe it is still best to go cautiously as if nothing critical had been established – for they would only cause more trouble if they spoke out about it. But which trouble are we most concerned with? Trouble for those believers who have not yet got strength from their faith to face what has been long established, or the trouble for would-be believers who cannot move nearer to faith as long as those believers are evidently so unreasonable and so fearful? I believe it to be my calling to face these issues openly and honestly, in the simple conviction that this is the way of faith and of mission.

Clearly, the heart of much of the outcry over my approach in these matters – both in the 'political' sphere and the area of biblical scholarship – lies with perceptions of the nature of authority. What authority do bishops have to make public pronouncements and what weight is the man in the street to give such pronouncements? This debate is not just about bishops but extends to the role of the Church in society, particularly the role of the Church of England because of its status as an Established Church with a recognised – if now largely nominal – place in the body politic.

Of the many letters sent to me between 1984 and 1986 some 4000 have been catalogued and studied. The assumptions they portray about what is expected of a bishop are interesting. They perhaps provide comfort in that there is obviously no consensus as to what defines proper episcopal behaviour. Four broad perceptions of bishops and the Church emerge:

A: A bishop is held to be a guardian of the faith, that is the upholder of tradition. His authority rests on his fidelity to tradition and the Church is defined as those who keep faith with a fixed body of received doctrine.

B: A bishop is a shepherd. His authority depends on the trust of his flock who must be gently led in noncontroversial consensus.

C: A bishop is a prophet and a judge. His role is to uphold moral judgements and his authority depends on his maintenance of a narrowly defined morality (principally personal and individual morality). In this understanding the Church is the people of God standing under a set of judgements fixed once and for all.

D: A bishop is an explorer. His role is to adapt religion to a new age and new circumstances. His authority lies in showing that faithfulness to the Tradition is expressed in relevance, both in applying it to what is going on and to judging what is going on. The Church is a dynamic vehicle for discovering new truths and adapting old wisdom to new circumstances.

I would argue that a bishop's role contains elements of all these, but one thing is clear, no one could hope to meet all these expectations. In the press, in particular, how each commentator defined the role of a bishop was crucial to the coverage of the first controversies and the coverage in turn shaped much of the public reaction. (A large number of the letters I received mention a mass media source – daily press, radio or television – as the basis of their knowledge or impression of my views.)

In an article in *The Times* published in April 1985, Clifford Longley wrote that a bishop's claim to authority rested on his role as 'guardian of the Christian faith'. He continued:

To be seen as having repudiated part of that faith is to lose all his authority, therefore, authority as a preacher of the Gospel on political and moral questions as much as a preacher of religious doctrine in the narrower sense. Conservative politicians of the Anglican obedience do not grant to the Bishops of Durham and Birmingham the right to criticise in the name of the Church, precisely because they have lost their authority. Both these Bishops have sometimes made controversial contributions to public debate on political issues, and both have made controversial contributions on theological issues. The link between the two is the issue of authority.

In this understanding of a bishop's role and authority (broadly corresponding to definition A found in the letters, but also present in definitions B and C), a bishop loses his authority to be taken seriously on any matter if he questions any of what are popularly conceived to be the 'received truths' of the Church. This would seem to reveal an alarmingly static and limited view of God who is apparently thought of as a personal possession whose purpose is to guarantee an individual's sense of security and an individual's peace of mind. Authority is to be related only to providing assurance and never to providing stimulus or creative disturbance. Authority is thus a means to serving personal security in a very individualistic form and goes with a high degree of dependency. This cannot be true. Christianity is a living Truth. It is not a matter of handing over packages of information with instructions about their application. Unless doctrines engage the responses of heart, soul and mind there is no point in speaking about them, and unless each believer can argue honestly for his or her beliefs in terms of present-day reality our faith is irrelevant. The more public anyone is in a representative capacity to do with God, Jesus and the Truth, the more it is essential to come clean – to be honest. A Church leader is trying to stand for the basic reality of God, the gracious response of God and the current availability of God. This means we are all set free to face things as they really are.

Therefore a Christian disciple must be devoted to truth and facing reality. But facing things as they really are is a confusing and troublesome business. Being realistic involves being honest about the controversies, conflicts and uncertainties that exist between and within human beings – in the Church as elsewhere. How should a bishop balance this with the demands that he be a 'focus of unity'? Which responsibility should take precedence – the responsibiliity to his understanding of God developed throughout his personal pilgrimage or the responsibility to the demands of his representative role as a Christian leader? Clearly he has to balance the two pressures, but in balancing them he must not cheat. That is, he must not pretend a particular inter-pretation is true and unassailable when it clearly is not. A bishop is not just a representative Christian. The role of the bishop is to expound the Faith, speaking from the inherited Tradition which is the record of faith through the ages. But he must also interpret that faith for the present day, for Tradition is a living thing. A bishop should share the Faith, to enable people who are already in it to go further in it, but also to put out hooks, probes, pins, prods among people who do not hold the Faith so that they may think about it again and see it as an option. A bishop is a shep-herd but a shepherd has to be part of dividing sheep from goats. A bishop has as much apostolic duty to proclaim the Kingdom as simply to keep people together. He is not there merely to rein-force opinions and positions already held; he should be provid-ing leadership or assistance in exploration, critical reassessment and discovery. Finally, he must speak of the judging element of God, reminding people that they are called to stand against those things which deny the worth of human beings and the love of God. No wonder there are so few model bishops about these days. Anyone called to the role must accept that there is no such thing as 'getting it right'. The most to be hoped for is to do one's best and depend on the Grace of God to make something of it.

The most serious charge made against me was that I was puncturing some people's faith by my approach. No Christian, let alone a Christian leader, can take such a charge lightly and I certainly do not. However, although I can understand that some people may have been distressed (and the style of reporting, or misreporting in some cases, must take some responsibility for the distress caused) I do not think that anyone who has a living faith, a praying and serving faith, could be put off by one person. The Bishop of Durham is only one bishop in one Church. The Church of England alone has over forty diocesan bishops. It is worth asking what kind of faith can be destroyed by the words of one man, whoever he is, and is such a faith real or just a set of propositions held in the mind?

One of the great dangers of religion is that people come to believe that it is there merely to give them comfort and protect them from reality. To protect oneself from reality is to build a wall between oneself and God. The purpose of religion is not to give people comfort. People should commit themselves to God and receive comfort. That is to say, the purpose of religion is to help people to get closer to God. In committing themselves to God, believers do find great consolation but if you are simply using religion to give yourself comfort then you are trying to make God a function of your needs and desires, whereas the great and glorious thing is that God is God. God who is much greater, much more lovely, much more lively, much more mysterious than we can imagine and it is He who puts life and personality into us.

There will always be people who seem determined to shut up the pursuit of things and powers spiritual within formulae and within institutions. They may well capture vantage points within religious institutions and will certainly be vociferous but this does not make them either typical or a majority. I might have found it hard to continue against the charges that I was damaging faith if I had not consistently received more signs of support than opposition. Signs such as the thousands of letters from people saying I was helping them and that I should continue. But more important than this is the question of what Christian Faith is for. It it just for Christians? Archbishop William Temple said that the Church is the one club which exists for people who are not its members. A tough ideal, but it represents a pressure to turn outwards. Turning outwards may well be away from those people who say: 'This is *my* faith; don't disturb it.' Such an attitude just does not begin to show the suffering exploration and caring of Jesus and, in its more extreme manifestations, does seem to support those critiques of religion and the Church – such as those of Marx and Durkheim – which claim to show that religion is more part of the sickness of humanity than of its health.

There is a passage from 1 Peter 3:15: 'Always be ready with an explanation for anyone who asks you for the grounds and shape of the hope that is in you in meekness and in fear, having a good conscience that, whereas they speak evil of you as of evil doers, they may be ashamed that falsely accuse your good conversation with Christ.' As I understand it, in this passage the author is saying that if you risk exploring the possibilities of humanity in the name of Jesus Christ, you will be as much a disturber – as much an obstacle and an offence – as a straightforward comforter. In a way he is saying, 'Don't be disturbed at being disturbing, but mind that you make the right sort of disturbance.' I continue in the hope that, by the Grace of God, I have made something like the right sort of disturbance.

Constitutionally I am not the sort of person who enjoys conflict and controversy. It can be a strange and disturbing experience to witness oneself being blackened, or cheapened or laughed off in the public media. In my case I was helped by the fact that it has always been clear to me that a bishop is a combination of a lightning conductor and a scapegoat. Also, Christians do have a model to handle uncomfortable periods of alienation or persecution. Neither Jesus nor Peter got away unscathed and although it would be foolish to claim an affinity, there is space in the Christian tradition to see persecution as an authenticating sign. To pick up a note sounded in 1 Peter 4:12 following: 'If these things come upon you, think what came upon Jesus or your brethren in the world.' Curiously enough, the reaction to the burning of York Minster gave some affirmation that I was on target in the right sort of battle. That is the battle about what God, if He exists, might be like. This is also the battle over the relationship of true religion to the supernatural and to magic on the one hand, and to some sort of 'true Godliness' on the other. So quite independent of feeling horrified at the burning of the Minster, the debate that surrounded the event had an oddly reinforcing effect. Most reinforcing of all was the fact that religion had been put back into its place as a common topic of conversation. As one of my Rural Deans pointed out, in a few months after I came to the diocese it got to be so clergy could not go out without having to discuss religion. However bumpy the ride, it has been a privilege to have been part of such a breaking out of the liveliness of faith.

So much for the grand scale – however, a bishop is not only a human being like all others but also has a practical daily life. In practical terms, the role of the bishop is threefold. He has to act as a sort of general manager and, in a sense, the focus of the administration of the running of the diocese. He has both to contribute to, and supervise, the pastoral care of the clergy. Then there is the teaching role. Tramping the diocese trying to help the people in the parishes to go deeper into things, helping them to be more excited about the Faith and supporting them in what they are doing. Thirdly, he has the position of being able to stand for the faith in public. This is part of making as clear as possible to the world outside that Christianity is something that engages with ordinary life and is important to everybody. From the beginning I felt that this last was at least as important as the other two strands. Although there were people in the public at large who seemed to think that I should stick to minding my own business (that is, what they thought to be the Church's business, whereas I imagined the Church's business to be God's business and therefore everybody's business), my diocese as a whole has taken this very well and been tremendously supportive.

Perhaps largely due to the flattering – if sporadic – attentions of journalists, I am sent a fair number of letters every week.

Unfortunately, periodically the numbers overwhelm me and I am not able to answer every one, and anyway non-urgent letters, I am ashamed to admit, routinely have to wait four weeks for a reply. Every now and then this produces an irate would-be correspondent who complains that surely a bishop should be pastoral enough, and courteous enough, to respond to his correspondents. Quite so, but sadly time, in this world at least, is not infinitely extendible. It became clear to me early on that very few people understand what a bishop actually does with his days. Many people seem to have a picture of a slightly Victorian figure sitting in his comfortable, book-lined study receiving the occasional cleric, writing the occasional sermon and perhaps composing a letter to *The Times* before driving out, accompanied by his chaplain, to do a little gentle confirming. I will admit to having a comfortable, book-lined study but there the resemblance ends.

It is hardly surprising that few people have a clear idea of what a bishop does. It is one occupation that does not come with a job description. Although in my time I have run time-management courses for bishops, I have to admit that I did not realise the full extent of the potential pressures on their time until I actually suffered the elevation myself.

To explode the first popular myth about bishops, the fact is that the day-to-day life of a Church of England bishop is as much managerial as spiritual. In Durham Diocese the bishop presides over 260 or so parishes and has the pastoral care of the 300 or so clergy who serve in them. It is not a particularly large diocese in numbers of parishes but geographically it is one of the more extensive ones in the Church of England – although with much splendid countryside travelling about is not too much of a chore. There is one suffragan bishop and we split the confirmations between us, doing about forty each every year. Most Sundays I visit a parish or two and each week there are extra services – perhaps to celebrate the anniversary or special feast day of a parish, or to institute a new vicar. I am not a great fan of committees but there are always the inescapable ones – perhaps one a week, or maybe two or three in a week at certain times of the year. There are also other engagements which are not strictly to do with church members but are in the community, such as visits to schools, addressing meetings of doctors, industrial managers, or teachers.

Being one of the senior bishops in the Church of England, the Bishop of Durham has a seat in the House of Lords. Because of the clash between the necessity to fix diocesan arrangements far in advance and the short-term notice given as to the timetable of debates in the House of Lords it is not possible to attend there very often. Nonetheless there is a need to keep up to date on the topical issues and occasionally trips down do have to be fitted in, particularly should a matter of local concern come up. There are civil ceremonies to take part in and the various openings and occasional dedications of libraries, schools, and sundry buildings. There are lectures and seminars to give, articles to write for religious and secular press. Innumerable letters to answer and quite a few to compose. I have a chaplain to assist me on diocesan administration, one full-time secretary, and my daughter acts as my external affairs assistant. Even with such a staff we never seem to be entirely on top of the workload.

I have been extremely lucky to have come to a diocese which has a splendid group of men and women working for it – from the Diocesan secretary, to Archdeacons, Rural Deans and parish ministry, both lay and ordained – without them my job would be impossible. My staff are very patient and I try hard to manage my time, fixing appointments and engagements in the afternoon and keeping the mornings clear to work on the ever-present backlogs of mail but it never quite seems to work out like that. At times I feel a great envy for Bishop Hensley Henson who, it seems, ordered his life much better than I do mine. He refused to have a telephone in the house so that one of many trials his chaplain had to undergo was to collect pennies for daily trips to the market place to make calls from a public telephone box. Bishop Henson obviously had a sensible attitude towards the proper pace of life – he had to be vigorously persuaded before he would even take to a car to get around the diocese. I take some consolation from my inability to keep up with my correspondence in the knowledge that many bishops have been famous for this failing. We had concrete proof of this when the main office was redecorated a few years back. In taking out some obsolete cupboards a drawer was unstuck and in it we discovered a bundle of unopened letters to the bishop. They were postmarked 1916.

3

Scripture and 'Literal Truth'

People who enjoy religion, like those who enjoy politics, have a
great love of labelling. I have been variously labelled in recent
years but one adjective I have rarely seen attached to my name is
'orthodox'. It may therefore appear strange to some that I personally classify myself within the Anglican Church – when I
must – as a 'critical orthodox'. To those sceptics who see me as
an innovating 'trendy' bishop, or even something of a heretic, I
would point out that my orthodoxy in essentials was sufficiently
recognised for me to have attended two Lambeth Conferences
as an official theological adviser long before I attended my third
as a bishop. (For the uninitiated, the Lambeth Conference is a
gathering held every ten years which draws together representative bishops from all parts of the Anglican Communion, that is
the Anglican churches around the world.) Yet I have been asked
several times over the last six years how I can recite the Creeds
at services in church, and have been told frequently by the
media and by individuals that I do not believe in the Resurrection or the Incarnation, two of the fundamental beliefs of the
Christian Church to which I belong.

However many times the public is told about the problems
and limitations of media reporting, some people, it seems, will
forever retain a child-like trust in the printed word. Perhaps it is
an effect of getting old, but I am continually amazed at the number of people who fail to question the source of what they have
read or even to apply moderate commonsense to weigh up the
likelihood of the truth of what is said. For instance, sometime in
1985 a leaflet began appearing up and down the country

distributed by an Islamic Propagation Centre in Birmingham. Its banner headline read: 'More than half of England's Anglican Bishops absolve themselves from Blasphemy and regard . . . JESUS AS ONLY A MESSENGER.' Then underneath, in a prominent position, was a rather unflattering picture of 'the Rev. Professor DAVID JENKINS'. The gist of the story was that I (along, it should be noted, with 'more than half of England's Anglican Bishops') rejected the divinity of Christ (that is, rejected the doctrine of the Incarnation) and his Resurrection. This leaflet, or versions of it, turned up all over the world and gave rise to many anguished accusations. Fellow Christians on the Indian continent and elsewhere wrote sorrowful and angry letters demanding to know if I was aware of how I was damaging the faith I was consecrated to protect. I, it seemed, had made a laughing-stock of my faith, my church and was quite probably in league with the devil into the bargain.

Very few of these correspondents were inclined to ask me what I had actually said. The story was such a temptingly awful one – a Christian bishop who publicly rejects the basics of his faith – that the very idea of it was worthy of wrath. Whether or not it was true, the Bishop of Durham must be to blame for allowing people to say such things of him. Temperate responses to the effect that such correspondents had been misled by false reports, tended to be countered along the lines of 'Well, you would say that now, wouldn't you?' There are some situations in which you cannot win. However, let me repeat myself.

I believe in the Resurrection of Jesus Christ Our Lord from the dead. I live in the hope of the Resurrection. I believe that Jesus Christ is both God for us and man with us. Anyone who says that I do not believe in the Resurrection and in the Incarnation is a liar. I say this fiercely and categorically because it means so much to me. However, if anyone wonders how I can believe in the Resurrection and the Incarnation and yet ask the questions I do, I shall try to explain.

I do not deny any basic Christian doctrines. What I have openly declared, and shall continue to maintain, is that literal belief in the Virgin Birth or the Empty Tomb are not basic Christian doctrines. The basic Christian doctrine is that God became Man in Jesus (in shorthand, the doctrine of the Incarnation). The story of the Virgin Birth is told to make that point. The basic Christian doctrine is that God raised up Jesus so that Jesus is alive for evermore. I have been trying to separate the basic Christian doctrines – in which I firmly believe – from the stories which have been told to get those doctrines over. The stories are very useful as a means of getting the point across, but only so long as people do not miss that point and get stuck on the stories.

The two theological issues which have caused most controversy in my case have been about how literally we are to understand the Virgin Birth references in the Gospels and the nature of Christ's raised body. The reason why people get so worked up about these details is because behind the argument lies a crucial debate over how to interpret the biblical texts. Christians often refer to the Scriptures as 'the Word of God', yet our great problem, from the very beginning, has always been how to interpret that Word. Many believers argue that to question those passages in the Gospels which support the literal interpretation of the Virgin Birth or the Empty Tomb is to question the Word of God and therefore must be unthinkable and outrageous. I believe that to expect to use the biblical texts in any simplistic and literal way is to misunderstand their nature, to demand the wrong sort of authority from them and implies a wholly wrong understanding of the God we know through Jesus.

We live in a culture much shaped by Christianity. Some familiarity with biblical stories, and attachment to what are understood to be traditional Christian beliefs, still extend beyond the group of practising Christians. This familiarity can be a disadvantage. Too often we think we know and therefore cease to test the truth of what we so vigorously and warmly maintain. At the time of one of the Easter fusses over my position on the Resurrection, *The Times* printed a letter from a then prominent member of our establishment. In it the writer stated that he preferred to believe the Evangelists on the subject of the Resurrection because 'they were there'. In fact it is well established that none of the Gospels was written until at least a generation after the events they record. In other words the writers were relying on reports, not direct personal experience, for their accounts of the life, death and Resurrection of Christ. They wove stories that had been told through the churches by the faithful into their Gospels, stories that may have been shaped through being part of the worship of the earliest churches. If we are to take historical truth seriously, believers have to accept that even in the Gospels there is some space between what the writers put down and the life of Christ. There are no eye-witness accounts. The earliest account of the Resurrection is in Paul's First Letter to the Corinthians and even here the writer was repeating accounts related to him by the leaders of the Church in Jerusalem.

Another complication we have to wrestle with is that Jesus did not speak Greek. The language he spoke was Aramaic, a Semitic language which was the local tongue in Palestine in his time. The Gospels we have often show echoes of Aramaic behind the Greek they are written in. Most scholars hold, however, that the Gospels were composed in Greek, even if there might have been one or two short Aramaic documents behind them. So we are already one language away from Jesus in the Gospel texts we have. These texts were later translated into various languages in the Ancient World and, eventually, into our modern European tongues. Nowadays there are a variety of translations in English. So although we have accounts of the things Jesus said, we do not have the actual words he spoke. Anyone who has tried learning a foreign language will know that this is not as trivial a point as it may sound. It is impossible for a text to undergo many translations from one language to another through the ages without there being shifts in meaning. Therefore, literal arguments from short texts chosen out of whichever translation one is using rest on very shaky ground.

Just as we have to live with shifts in the meaning of words, so we have to live with shifts in our understanding of history. In the Old City in Jerusalem there is a Convent of the Sisters of Zion. When I first went there, some twenty years ago, it was generally believed that the pavement in their basement was part of the Antonia fortress of Herod's and therefore of Jesus's time.

So it was thought it would very likely be the pavement mentioned in John, Chapter 19 (called, in Greek, Lithostrotos), on which Pilate set up his judgement seat. People pointed to a carved game on the stone – the board for a dice game called 'the King's Game' found all over the Roman world. There you could imagine, it was said, the soldiers gambling for Jesus's clothes. On the evidence of the time I found this site one of the most moving places in Jerusalem. Here I felt as if I stood where Our Lord's feet had stood. But archaeologists and scholars worked on and it was discovered a few years back that the pavement, and the splendid arch called the Ecce Homo around which the Convent chapel is built, were in fact constructed in Hadrian's time, some 100 years after Pilate.

I use this as an acute example of the way in which every time you try to pin the stories of the Gospels down to places or literal interpretation, it cannot be done. This does not mean that events did not happen. You can visit the general area where Jesus lived and preached in His earthly life. You can pick up echoes of how it must have been, but we cannot pin our faith to particular historical details or particular words in a text.

At this point I hear the despairing cry – 'If that is so, what are we left with?' I firmly believe there is absolutely no need to panic. What we are left with is the reliable witness of faithful and inspired men and women to the impact of Jesus, the faith he inspired and the sort of things he said. People have to get used to what a human book the Bible is. It contains all sorts of exciting things that are put in all sorts of different ways. We are not called to be too literal minded about it, we have to be realistic and faithful about it.

The approach of critical scholarship to the Bible does not destroy its validity, it releases its power from the deep freeze, sets it in motion, allowing it to live. Critical scholarship engages the vital human factor: the essential response of individual persons and communities – today as in the past – to the God reflected in the Scriptures. The Scriptures are written from faith for faith, and depend on the Holy Spirit and our response to be living and lively aids to faith.

To believe that the writers of the Gospels were assisted by

God, does not have to mean that God guided or assisted in such a way as to blot out the personal contribution of the writer or to make what he wrote infallible. The writers of the New Testament had simple faith and simple purpose but they were also complicated people affected by their time. We should be able to enter dialogue with them and in this be taken into the heart of their faith.

In one particular interview, a year or two ago, I was faced by a rather angry lady journalist (who, as I recall, was keen to point out she was not a believer) who claimed that by calling the Gospel stories symbolic I was implying that the Gospel writers were liars. If you read religious literature right up until at least the eighteenth century, people were not liars for telling symbolic stories. They told stories they believed to reflect a mysterious truth. To imagine that the Gospel writers set down their accounts in something approaching the journalistic manner of today is simply a mistake which shows a lack of understanding and imagination. The Ancients had a much greater sense of poetry and mystery in their religious witness than believers have shown for the most part in modern times. The Gospel writers knew that they were dealing with mysteries, so they were quite prepared to tell stories with a bit of dimension in them where you could get into the Mystery. The tragedy in shutting the Bible down to the literal level is that you shut out the space which tells of the Mystery. The Evangelists, Matthew, Mark, Luke and John, wrote with the presence of the Spirit but they must not be imagined as merely taking dictation from God. We need to accept that from our very earliest sources we are dealing with constructions of faith.

According to the present consensus of modern scholarships, Mark's Gospel, the shortest of the four, is the earliest. Matthew and Luke took over Mark's account, edited it, and added to it, interpreting his material to suit the needs of different Christian communities. John's Gospel has a very different feel to the other three. The writer thinks in pictures and symbols and tends to have three different meanings for everything he says. His style is something like one of those television programmes where the screen is full of the main narrative but then in one quarter of the screen another film is imposed. This, perhaps, points up the message the commentator is drawing out from the scene in the main frame, or it might suggest – maybe in a flashback – what is going on in the mind or life of a character in the main picture.

For example, John writes of the 'Last Supper' quite differently from Matthew, Mark and Luke. This is the meal Jesus shared with his disciples before he was arrested, tried and crucified. In Matthew, Mark and Luke, Jesus shares bread and wine with his disciples and relates this to the meaning of his coming death. It is these stories of the Last Supper on which the 'Holy Communion' services of the Christian churches are based. But John has no report of this. Instead he does two things. Firstly, earlier in his Gospel (Chapter 6) John has a long series of discussions in which Jesus speaks about feeding and says things like: 'I am the bread of life.' It is all about the same thing as the Last Supper stories. In doing this John is offering commentary and explanation coming from later reflection, meditation and inspiration. Then, secondly, in the place where the other three Gospels have stories of the Last Supper, John has the equally famous story of Jesus acting as a slave and washing the feet of his disciples. This is another powerful piece of enacted symbolism about Jesus on the way to his death. He is the servant of all and he is about to save them by giving himself in obedience and death. As John has Jesus say: 'The bread which I will give is my own flesh; I give it for the life of the world' (John 6:51). John is clearly sharing the same faith with writers of the other Gospels and is putting over the same message about Jesus. He is simply putting things in a very different way.

So the authors of the Gospels of Matthew, Luke and John did not treat the Gospel of Mark in what we would call a simply literal or factual way. They felt quite free to retell stories, to relocate them, to add or subtract details in order to give a particular slant to the particular message in relation to the overall Gospel which they felt called to present.

Take the story of the draught of fishes. Matthew and Mark tell how Jesus calls Peter, Andrew and the sons of Zebedee on the shore of the Lake of Galilee and tells them that they will become fishers of men (Mark 1:17; Matthew 4:19). Luke, in Chapter 5, picks up this story and turns it into an occasion when the disciples take in a miraculous draught of fishes which makes Peter say to Jesus: 'Depart from me for I am a sinful man', and the net breaks because of the sheer weight of the catch. But if you turn to John's Gospel the story is no longer located in the period when Jesus begins his public ministry and calls his disciples. In John this incident is told as part of the Resurrection narratives (John, Chapter 21). In his version the net does not break and Peter is commissioned to go out and preach the Gospel. If we are going to be free to believe we have got to understand that the major preoccupation of the Gospel writers was not to give accurate and historical accounts as we would understand them. What they are talking about is faith and encounter; meeting Jesus in his ministry and then meeting the risen Jesus and being ready to go out and serve him.

The virginal conception of Jesus is described in the first two chapters of Matthew and in the first chapter of Luke. It is not mentioned by the other two Evangelists. It is not clear how far Matthew and Luke themselves meant the story to be taken at face value. For example, they both include genealogies of Jesus – in Matthew tracing his descent from Abraham and in Luke from Adam – both of which involve descent through the male line of Joseph. This would seem to imply that Joseph was understood to be Jesus's biological father. Further, the two genealogies do not agree with one another. They are making a point about Jesus symbolically and not literally.

If we are to take scholarship seriously, we must also consider things like the following. In writing about the Virgin Birth, Matthew uses a text from the prophet Isaiah in the Old Testament. 'Behold a virgin shall be with child and shall bring forth a son and they shall call his name Emanuel, which being interpreted is, God with us' (Matthew 1:23). Matthew wrote this down in Greek and his quotation comes from a Greek translation of the Hebrew in which Isaiah's prophecy was originally written. In the Greek version there is the word 'parthenos' – which certainly usually means 'maiden' or 'virgin'. But in the Hebrew (Isaiah 7:14) the original word used simply means 'young woman'. Indeed, our New English Bible translates the verse in the Old Testament 'a young woman is with child'. As I have already said, translations can shift meanings.

This all sounds rather complicated, especially as it also introduces us to the way writers in the New Testament re-use texts from the Old Testament. They tend to give the old texts a meaning which fits into the interpretation they are after as *New* Testament writers. This seemed a perfectly proper procedure to them, for they believed that what God had been in Jesus, and what God had done in Jesus, carried on what God had shown Himself to be and do in the Old Testament. This means that texts cannot prove as we think of proof. They communicate discoveries of faith. They indicate continuity. They speak of how unexpectedly new things come out of the old. They are used in good faith to share lively faith.

To return to the particular matter of the Virgin Birth – if we are honest with ourselves we must face the fact that there are important and disturbing implications in a rigid insistence on a literal Virgin Birth. Obsession with virginity carries some pretty dangerous baggage. It is an emphasis which developed as the Church moved out into the Greek world. It does not fit into the Hebrew-based world of the Bible with its strong affirmation of family life and normal sexuality. False obsessions lead us into dangers of distortion and confusion. For example, Mary is supposed to be the mother figure and yet she is represented as a virgin. No wonder Christians have been known to get into a terrible muddle over sex and the place and role of women. We need to consider the possibility that this is yet another area where we have misinterpreted the Word of God. A misinterpretation which, I believe, comes from a literal approach which is not appropriate to the way people originally wrote and used the texts.

I know that many people find great difficulty in doing without a literal interpretation of the Virgin Birth stories. They feel that it is required if God is really one with Man in Jesus. I do not believe that this follows at all. In my understanding, God in Jesus is so down to earth He chose to take on all the risks and realities of becoming human. To interfere in natural human processes would therefore seem unnecessary and not in line with the God who works in reality.

If you take a fresh look at the birth stories you will see that they have a particular style which distinguishes them from the rest of the Gospels. They read like well-crafted stories fitted together by Matthew and Luke to make the points they were inspired to make. These stories are full of echoes of the Old Testament. As I have already pointed out, these older passages are given special meaning in relation to Jesus. The stories act in Matthew and Luke as their introductions to the miracle of this man Jesus. There are serious critical and historical grounds for treating the story as one of the very early embroideries added to express the wonder of the discovery that this Jesus is God for us.

Given this position of mine on the literal interpretation of the Virgin Birth, I am sometimes asked how I can recite the Creeds in church with a clear conscience. After all, one of them says of Jesus: 'born of the Virgin Mary' and the other says, 'and was incarnate by the Holy Ghost of the Virgin Mary, and was made Man'. I find no problem with this. I firmly believe in the Incarnation. I believe that Jesus is the Saviour of Mankind. It is also clear to me that the early chapters of Luke and Matthew contain stories which have been made up out of bits of the Old Testament and traditions that emerged about Jesus after he had been raised from the dead and believers knew for certain that he was the Son of God. So I can, with an open mind and a clear conscience, recite in a church service a Creed which stands as the symbol of the Church's belief in Jesus Christ. Belief today not only requires some grasp of the realities of history and critical study but also an understanding that the Bible offers much of its greatest truth through symbolic stories, poems and hymns of praise.

I recite the Creeds as poems to the glory of God. These poems have emerged in the history and experience of the Church from real experiences of God in Jesus and through the Spirit. If you want to take each little bit apart, then each individual has to go away into a corner and discuss them in depth with fellow Christians to see what it means to them. But you must be careful. Once you start taking the Creed to pieces – just as when you try to take verses of the Bible out of context – it is rather like dissecting a piece of cut glass. Separate out the facets from one another and they cease to reflect the mysterious inner fire.

I hope I have made it clear that I do not consider a belief in the literal Virgin Birth necessary to the doctrine of the Incarnation nor to Christianity. However, belief in the Resurrection certainly is a fundamental doctrine of Christianity. The media report which, in my case, most stood truth on its head was the one which stuck me with the popular tag of being the bishop who said that the Resurrection was 'a conjuring trick with bones'. In fact, I said precisely the opposite. The occasion was an in-depth, and fairly select, discussion programme on the Resurrection, hosted by Radio 3. In the midst of a lively debate I responded to another participant, who seemed to be arguing for a narrowly physical interpretation of the Resurrection, by saying that surely the Resurrection was clearly much more than just a conjuring trick with bones. What I was trying to underline was that the Resurrection is the raising up of the person of Jesus in his wholeness and his completeness so that he is alive for evermore. That is much more than the reanimation of a corpse – more than just flesh and bones. It is something spiritual for eternity.

Some argue that you can 'prove' the Resurrection by the fact that the Tomb was empty on that first Easter Day. Firstly, at this distance you cannot prove such a thing; the physical details must remain a mystery. Secondly, even if you could prove that the Tomb was empty, what would it mean? Does it not imply a frag-ile belief that rests on very little? Just suppose some archaeolo-gist some day dug up another tomb in Jerusalem. Suppose that with carbon dating or whatever techniques this archaeologist convinced scientists that this tomb was indeed the Tomb of Christ. Then, just suppose, the archaeologist also found bones which were reasonably held to be the bones of Christ. Would such a discovery disprove the Resurrection. Surely not. What I know is that Jesus was dead; Jesus was buried; and people became convinced that Jesus was alive and I believe with them. An Empty Tomb proves nothing and can itself not be proved.

Believers have to stop expecting the Bible to be as literal as our modern journalistic reports. The traditional gospel for Easter Sunday has a note of puzzlement and unfinished business about it. The earliest trustworthy manuscripts of Mark's Gospel, the earliest of the four Gospels, ends abruptly at Chapter 16, Verse 8. This finds the women at the tomb and ends 'they said nothing to anybody for they were afraid'. Yet still people today continue to want to be certain and sure about the precise details. They produce little books which attempt to show that the different stories in the Gospels about the Resurrection can be reconciled with one another and that the Resurrection can be 'proved'. They seem to feel that they have to be sure about mechanics in order to believe the Resurrection. But the Resurrection is so wonderful you can never be sure about the mechanics – only that it was reality that happened. What we have is the evidence of the people who bore witness years after and have continued to do so right around the world throughout the ages. The question is, do we trust them?

I do. I share the faith of the apostles and I follow St Paul's account of the Resurrection. St Paul was clear that the Resurrection body was not a physical one. In Chapter 15 of his first letter to the Corinthians, Paul meditates at length on what our resurrection will be like. His words clearly reflect how he also thinks of the Resurrection of Christ. At one point he says: 'but some men will say, how are the dead raised up? And with what body do they come? Thou fool . . .' (15:35). Then he goes on with his discussion. Obviously he thinks it is stupid to be literal minded about physical bodies when thinking, and hoping, about the Resurrection.

Given the reaction of some people to my remarks about the Empty Tomb and the nature of the raised body, much of the problem seems to lie in language. To give an illustration. One gentleman who happens to disagree with my position, tells a story about a friend of his who is a bulb grower. The gentleman has his friend say that he is pleased the Bishop of Durham says that a spiritual Resurrection is better than a physical one for now, when his bulbs fail to come up, he can write a letter to disappointed customers that 'you have had a better resurrection than flowering because they have come up spiritually'. In this view, if you maintain Christ's Resurrection is a spiritual one then God is definitely disappointing His customers. If you imagine the 'physical' to represent the essence of personality and to be the only thing that is really real, then a 'spiritual' Resurrection may sound all too airy-fairy and a bit of a cheat. But this is not the orthodox Christian understanding. In the Christian sense, 'spiritual' indicates what is truly real and lasting – the essence of personality, the spirit – whereas the 'physical' represents the earthly embodiment and expression of us as persons.

Discussions of this sort naturally touch off a whole series of human fears about the after-life and whether we continue as ourselves. As we only really know ourselves in our human bodies we tend to be rather attached to them and very much identify ourselves with our physical shape. I do not know whether we retain our shape into the after-life. Besides, if we do, at which age? Do those who die in their eighties totter around heaven with their infirmities intact? Do we assume the body of the age at which we were most happy in life? (You can imagine the angst of arriving in heaven to discover that your mother was happiest aged two!) We cannot know the answer, it is a mystery. All I do know is that I am so convinced of the power and reality of God's love, as shown above all in the Resurrection of Jesus Christ, that I believe we can be taken by God after death into something infinitely worthwhile. As to details, we can only trust in God.

This has always been the case for believers. The very first Christians came to understand the Resurrection gradually, through a whole number of partial insights and encounters. Encounters such as the two friends who were travelling to Emmaus. It was only when they stopped to break bread that they discovered that Jesus was going with them. They came to believe that they had to go out and preach and teach and heal. This was what the Resurrection meant.

It is the second generation of Christians who started the process of exaggeration. By the time the Gospels were written there were all kinds of miraculous stories going around. The Easter stories in the Gospels have elements of what we would call propaganda. To show how earth-shattering it all was, people started talking about earthquakes. So Matthew had an earth-quake to mark the Resurrection. The first disciples did not need such supporting miracles. They simply knew the central and basic miracle of Jesus Christ raised from the dead.

It has always been abundantly clear to me that Christianity could never have arisen unless the first disciples had been turned into apostles by the discovery, conviction and assurance that God had raised Jesus from the dead. Ever since I have been a self-conscious and reflective Christian, I have been absolutely clear that being a Christian means believing that the first disciples were right in their belief. God did indeed raise Jesus from the dead. The issue, therefore, is not 'did the Resurrection happen?', still less, 'in what way did the Resurrection happen?'. The issue is 'what does the Resurrection mean?' But before I go on with exploring this central issue of the Resurrection at work in the world, I need to take a look at the way people think about God at work in the world. Our ideas about God and the world are too often, both for believers and unbelievers, confined and confused by notions about miracles.

4

The Laser Beam God

◆

We need, therefore, to discuss miracles and mystery. I realise that this is something of a conversation-stopper. God is a mystery, miracles are part of that mystery, so surely all discussion stops here. Or, at least, all further discussion is nothing but hot air. It is all a matter of simple faith. It is futile to question mystery. Simple faith is best. The Bishop of Durham does not have simple faith; he questions mysteries and miracles, therefore he does not believe; it is as simple as that. In fact, I do believe in miracles. My problem is neither with miracles nor mystery but with the way self-confessed believers sometimes misunderstand and misuse miracles and mystery.

God is a Mystery. Each individual believer gets on to God through a different set of pictures, experiences and ideas that reflect that Mystery. For some the Empty Tomb says it all; for others the Cross is the key; for others particular personal encounters provide the catalyst that puts them on to God. The difficulty is that however personally important these pictures, experiences and ideas are – however much they support our individual faith – they do not encapsulate God. Believers are forever mistaking the things which get them on to God for absolutes. Whatever we know, God is still a Mystery and we are still inadequate to encompass truth. Because we are not big enough to face the risk, challenge and enormity of the Mystery, we tend to grasp for certainties and irrefutable signs. We have to be clear-eyed about this failing or else we get stuck on the wrong things intead of keeping our eyes on God.

Jerusalem gives an illustration of what I am getting at. The city of Old Jerusalem is full of religious signs of believers in the one God. There are minarets for the Muslims, church domes for the Christians, synagogues for the Jews. Deep in the Old City you find the Church of the Holy Sepulchre almost buried among the tightly packed buildings – it is the mosque nearby that stands out. Surrounded by a tangle of twisting Arab streets the Church itself is a remarkable jumble. Historically it is extremely interesting. The present building incorporates the remains of rock tombs from the first century AD, bits of the façade date from Crusader times, and if you have the energy you can descend deep into a cave where people have claimed from the fifth century that the Empress Helena found the true Cross. In some ways it is religiously remarkable too – so many people have arrived there over the centuries to say their prayers. When people do that over a significant time it does seem to make a difference.

Why do these pilgrims come to this Church of the Holy Sepulchre? Because it contains a first-century tomb which has been venerated for centuries as the tomb of Christ and, to the right as you come in the main door, there is a rock which is said to be Calvary, the place of the crucifixion. Apart from simple tourists, many Christians come to the place where, they believe, Christ died and the tomb from which he rose again can be seen. Standing in line before the rather tawdry tabernacle that now covers the Holy Sepulchre, waiting to visit the famous tomb, I cannot help asking myself: 'So what?' Supposing we did know for certain that this was the tomb of Christ. Supposing we knew for certain that the women found the tomb empty on the first Easter Day. What would it show? It would show that something mysterious had happened. Perhaps it would show that something rather nasty had happened – the body had been taken. But does it matter? After all, what was the punchline to that story? 'He is not here. He is risen!'

It is quite possible, gazing around, to imagine that the importance given to the place is damaging. All the different Christian churches in the Holy Sepulchre – the Greek Orthodox, the Catholics, the Armenians, the Copts – have spent centuries quarrelling over who should control which bit of what Holy

Shrine. They even quarrelled over who should maintain certain walls, being prepared to let them almost fall down rather than allow one church to claim another inch of wall by mending it. Even today bits of the building are rather shabby. The squabbling got so bad that for a long time the gentleman who kept the key to the building had to be a Muslim. And what was all this fighting about? Even if this was the tomb of Christ – He is not here. He is risen!

A few hours spent in the half-light and jumble of the Holy Sepulchre meditating on how we religious people get things so wrong, can be rather depressing. Yet I am also reminded that God in Jesus plunged himself into the ambiguity of the human world; the ambiguity crucified him and finished him but he rose again. The excitement of the Resurrection is all around, but not very much, I fear, in many of our so-called 'holy' places. Despite the mess and muddle we make of things, God goes on being alive and raising things up.

Yet still human beings keep trying to pin God down. Near the bus station in Jerusalem, down a narrow street between high stone walls, is what is called the Garden Tomb. Late in the nineteenth century, General Gordon and others discovered this site as the tomb of Jesus. Many Victorians much preferred this garden tomb to the inner-city site of the Holy Sepulchre. It looked so much better. Near by, there is a hill which can be said to be skull-like which fitted in with references in the Scriptures. Take a tour these days and guides will point out the wine press, the grove of trees, and tell you how this fits with biblical descriptions of a quiet garden outside the walls of the city. Many people believe that here they are in touch in a material way with the earthly presence of Christ and feel supported and refreshed in this green garden. Does it really matter that archaeological evidence cannot support the authenticity of this site, or of any other? If some simple believers find General Gordon's site a comfort, do they not have a right to enjoy that comfort?

Of course they have a right to enjoy this garden but we have to beware of being misled by our own imagery. There is nothing wrong in reconstructing images from the accounts in the Bible so long as we do not then expect the Christian Faith to lead us to quiet gardens and tranquillity. At the gate of the garden tomb a bomb killed a tourist not so long ago. The stone walls around the bus station are covered with slogans reflecting the strife and misery of the Intefada. This is the real world into which God came down to earth in Jesus; the world that crucified Him and this is the reality He wrestles with still.

The God of the Bible is not a tranquil God. He is more often than not a disturbing God. Abraham was pushed out from his home until he came to Bethel and met God under a palm tree. There is no indication that Abraham found being discovered by God a comfortable experience. No only did he have to leave his home but he was tested in a most disturbing way in relation to his precious son, Isaac, being convinced at one time that he was asked to sacrifice him. As it says in Hebrews 11, faith helped Abraham to go through many trials for God, but it was clearly a very disturbing relationship. 'By faith Abraham obeyed the call to go out to land destined for himself and his heirs and left home without knowing where he was to go.' The story of God and His dealings with men and women is not about finding truths and preserving them, it is always about moving on. Prophets going to people and calling them, trying to give messages which are not always heard or understood. The story of the people of God is definitely not a secure or comfortable one. Think of Moses. He left a life of pampering at Pharaoh's court – and for what? To be caught up in an exodus to a promised land which he never quite got to.

Jesus and the prophets constantly called people's ordinary, simple, unquestioning religion into question so that they could go deeper and become more open to God. There is nothing in the Bible that suggests that God gathers people up into a comfort which is unquestioning. The comfort believers receive from God is the sort of strength that enables you to go through the valley of the shadow of death. We must be very careful about insisting that either individuals, groups or even 'the Church' hold absolute truths. Believers must always be on a pilgrimage towards greater truth. Too much religion is far too small. The Father of Jesus is the God of the whole earth and the pilgrimage of faith is about so much more than just our petty truths and concern for our own comforts or fears.

So what about miracles? Where do they fit in? Many people who proclaim themselves believers in God set enormous store by miracles and hold that miracles are central to faith in God. As they are part of the Mystery we cannot dissect miracles but we may well ask why they happen. Are miracles proofs, are they rewards or are they gifts? The question we can, and must, ask ourselves is what do our belief in, and expectations of, miracles say about our picture of God? For how you understand miracles is an important reflection of what it is like to believe in God and how God works in the world.

In 1986 I made a speech to the General Synod of the Church of England in connection with debate over a document entitled 'The Nature of Christian Belief'. In that speech I raised the question of what sort of God we were portraying and believing in if we insisted on (as I then put it) 'the divine laser beam' type of miracle as the heart and basis of the Incarnation and the Resurrection. That is, in order for the Incarnation and Resurrection to be believable, real and historical, did God have to intervene in the manner of something like a divine laser beam, fusing the physical particles into a new reality which was both divinely produced and divine? This raises the other side of the proper literal interpretation of the Bible argument I went into in the last chapter. I have already discussed my reasons for believing that it is a simple misreading of the Gospel writers to insist on a literal Virgin Birth (that is, Jesus conceived by direct divine intervention and no human father) or a literal physical understanding of the Resurrection (that is, a Resurrection of which the reanimation of Jesus's earthly corpse was a crucial part). The other side of this debate is: what sort of God are we portraying if we believe He works His power in the world in this literal, knock-down way?

Before I go on I think I ought to make a brief detour. After my Synod speech in the summer of 1986 I was reported in some quarters as having said that not only did I not believe in miracles, the Resurrection or the Incarnation, but that God was a cultic idol. So it can be assumed that I am profoundly conscious of the dangers of pursuing the following arguments. Misunderstandings easily arise, people are not always good at listening, and some people do not want to listen anyway. I do not always express myself all that clearly and some of the questions are difficult. However, if, as I believe, God took on risk in Creation I suppose I must take it on in life. Still, may I first restate for the record that I do believe in miracles, the Resurrection and the Incarnation. Furthermore, I believe the one true God I know through Jesus Christ not only is, but is God and He does not remotely resemble a cultic idol (and that, indeed, is the whole point).

It seems all too often to be assumed that if God is 'God Almighty' then He must act, at least on significant occasions, in 'knock-down' ways. The basic picture, implied or explicit, is of God the Almighty King. All-mightiness meaning wholly irresistible in a take-it-or-leave-it way which flattens all opposition. It therefore follows that miracles are conceived of as a localised and controlled explosion of that sort of power. God being irresistibly God and making clear that He is irrefutably God. So here we have two things about miracles:

1 that they can be seen as important – or even the principal – evidence that God exists and that He is God (that is, miracles as 'proof').
2 that the sort of power God wields in the world – when He chooses to do so – is the irresistible kind.

If the miracles of the Resurrection and the Incarnation indicate that physical transformation through precise and overwhelming intervention is an option taken by God, consistent with His character revealed in the Bible, then believers are faced with a terrible dilemma. That is, that this God Christians call the God of Love is prepared to work knock-down physical miracles in order to let a select number of people into the secret of His Incarnation and Resurrection but He is not prepared to use those same methods in order to deliver victims from Nazi death camps, or to prevent Hiroshima or to overcome famine. If such perceptions are correct then such a god must be a cultic idol. A cultic idol is an imagined god who is supposed solely to benefit the people who believe in him, the worshippers who make up his cult. This is a distorted and misdeveloped picture of the true and gracious God. A distorted picture, furthermore, drawn by would-be worshippers who have gone dangerously and sadly astray. Such a god would not be worth believing in. It is a good thing that this is not the God pointed to in the Bible.

Christians believe that Jesus is the Christ of God and therefore rightly recognised by the Church as being 'of one substance with the Father'. This means that Jesus is our central key to the nature of God. The life of Jesus recounted in the Gospels shows us that God is not an imperial Caesar god of knock-down power, but a creative servant God of invincible love.

The answer to questions such as, how could a loving God allow such things as the Nazi death camps to take place, lies in the fact that we have got the concept of God's power wrong. I do not believe that God could stop what happened in Auschwitz. He could not, or He would have. God is not omnipotent in that way. He took a risk in creating man in His own image, which means that man was given freedom. If man has freedom then God cannot be omnipotent, if by omnipotent we mean that God is some great celestial emperor who has everything right under His control. It is blatantly obvious, if you just take a look at history and our present times, that the world is not like that and God is not like that.

To say that God is not omnipotent seems to indicate that He is so limited that He has no control or purpose. This is wrong. Jesus teaches us that God's control and purpose is the purpose of Love. Whatever happens, Love – as symbolised by Christ on the Cross suffering through the point of death itself – has the capacity to suffer and go through anything. Such is the invincibility of God. This is where, especially after such evils as the Holocaust and Auschwitz, I believe Christians must rethink very deeply and painfully about our image of God and how He works. Such a reassessment is baffling and frightening but it must be gone through if believers are to be realistic about the world as it is and continue to develop in faith and hope.

The miracles of this God we know in Jesus are never knock-down or obvious; there will always be another way of interpreting or explaining miraculous happenings. Miracles can be perceived and identified only by personal faith within the tradition, story and community of faith. This is not to say that miracles are only subjective experiences. It means that God does not force Himself on people. He offers Himself to us for our response, obedience and collaboration.

To look at it another way. We often hear of miracles these days in ways which seem to reduce them to the level of part of the currency of people who use religion. Tales of people praying for a parking space or a new washing machine. I cannot escape the conclusion that to reduce the miracles of the God represented in the Bible to the level of finding parking spaces for the select is absurd. It is simply not the case either in biblical records, or in the subsequent history of the world and of the Church, that God works manipulative and compelling miracles. God is not a 'fixer' or provider of comforts for His favoured few. Just look at the biblical accounts. Despite miracles the people of God have evidently gone on suffering and sinning alongside the celebrations.

There is much in-talk and claims about miracles which smack of paganised religion. The way some people seem to approach God and Jesus is reminiscent of the behaviour of those 'believers' who built temples around the Mediterranean to Apollo or some other deity. A deity who, if you burn incense to him, crawl on your knees in the right way and keep your fingers crossed, just might reward you; although there are no guarantees. This deity has his own odd ways of doing things. This is treating the God of Jesus on the Cross as if He were one of those idols which have been around ever since man gained a sense of the supernatural.

It seems that we have got the picture of God all wrong. It is much more likely that God has taken on the risk of creation, leaving a space in which miracles may happen but they are not the kind of knock-down 'reward' or 'proof' interventions that are decisive for all with eyes to see.

Miracle comes from the Latin word 'miracula' meaning wonderful works. 'Miraculum' is a thing which makes you wonder. So a miracle is a wonder whereby people get on to God especially and personally, and are very often changed by it. I stress here not only the person factor but also the response. Miracles are not occasions where God intervenes willy-nilly, upsetting the natural order of things to such an extent that the example may be held up as proof to all of His power. A miracle, like God, can never be pinned down.

You can receive something that happens to you as a miracle, as a special message of God to you, but it is a message which helps you to wonder about God and to be part of the wonder of God. The God of the Bible does not protect his followers from reality. Miracles do not transform history or reality in publicly obvious ways. It may be only after an event that you look back and see that God has been with you, and that now you have been given the chance to do something with God and for God now. Or you might be jolted by something that makes you think about things in a different way. However much you are sup-ported or helped, miracles are always to be taken as personal gifts for what follows. They are not to be taken as guarantees that God will give a repeat performance.

The desire for absolute and clear signs as proof that God exists, is nothing new. From the very beginning Jesus was up against those who wanted displays of knock-down power – the Church and Christians have always been drawn towards the mirage of the emperor god. However, Jesus, Lord and Saviour on behalf of the Servant God, expressed caution about 'signs and wonders'. In the Temptation narratives he is portrayed as refusing to contemplate turning stones into bread in order to convince the disbelieving. He warns against those who demand 'proof miracles' ('except you see signs and wonders you will not believe', John 4:48). At the crucifixion the mockers demand: 'Let Christ the King of Israel descend now from the Cross that we may see and believe.' But there was no coming down from the Cross that everyone might believe – believe what? That God was the Tyrant of Tyrants, the irresistible Emperor of Emper-ors? The central, original, wonderful message of Jesus was and is that there is another way. That the power of God is the strength of invincible Love.

This is all very well, I can hear you say, but what about what the Church teaches, what about Tradition? The Church and Tradition, we are told, hold that Christians should accept the literal, knock-down miracles of the Virgin Birth and the physical Resurrection. Look at the Bible. There are many instances of miraculous knock-down interventions by God. Yes – that is the picture of God which people formed in biblical times. The living God got in touch with them through these pictures. Can and should these pictures be ours? This is what the argument and exploration is all about. What they had, and what we have, is the opportunity to trust God. Christians do not believe in the Bible or in religious doctrines as defined by the Church; they believe in God. It should never be forgotten that religion saves no one. It is God who saves. Religion, and what religious people say, has often been against God.

The Old Testament itself makes it quite clear that one of God's perpetual problems has always been with His believers and their picture of Him. As it says in the Book of Micah: 'the Lord has a controversy with his people'. In the New Testament Paul makes clear in his Epistles that from the very beginning Christians have disagreed about all sorts of things. I would not be able to believe in God at all if the Bible were not full of examples in which God sends prophets to condemn the very way in which people think that they are responding to Him. God clearly does have a controversy with His people. Religion is as much a matter to be critical about as anything else. This is where responsibility and the use of reason comes in. False simplicities which ignore facts, and which often lead to mistreating people, are bad simplicities.

The Bible makes it clear that there has always been good and bad religion. If women and men in God's Image have freedom, they also have the ability to get things wrong and this does not cease merely because human beings gather together in a church. None of us is a consistent advantage to God. I must get in His way at times; we all do. This is the point about grace, forgiveness and the down-to-earthness of God. God took on all these failures and this sinfulness on the Cross and Jesus's Resurrection proved that even our sins and constant falling short cannot get Love down.

God entices us to go on risking, to go on hoping and daring to explore. We have to keep checking up with the help of fellow Christians, and other fellow human beings, as to whether we are taking risks in the wrong direction or in a good and positive direction. No Christian can let themselves off working things out for themselves and just rely on what the Church says. The Church of God is not primarily an institution; it is a living body of the people of faith and these people of faith are forever moving forwards. Faith is not just a pilgrimage for individual Christians, the Church is part of the pilgrimage too. There is no possibility of fixing God down in some magic formula and then sitting back and guarding it religiously.

The whole business of belief in God is to do with what you can pick up in the midst of the mess human beings so often get themselves into. It is not a question of finding answers to everything. A true picture of God – not the limited picture of an omnipotent and arbitrary emperor God – leads us to realise that believing in God is not a matter of providing 'answers' to things like the terrible events that take place in the world, but helping us to live with them and believing that there is more in the positive, worthwhile side of existence than in the negative, destructive side of human existence.

Being faithful to Tradition means thinking about the central mysteries of the faith in a way that takes full account of where we are now in our contemporary world. The received Tradition of the Church is about God, about God being with us in Jesus, about God being with us now. It is not about God being tied up in any particular packages – be they stories or doctrines or past history. Believers should spend more time examining their assumptions about God. Too often He is talked about as if He were an elderly, rather bossy man, who dwells mainly in the past. A God who froze somewhere between the first and fourth centuries. God is not some extraterrestrial being who switched off at approximately AD 90, flashed on around the time of Luther and has switched off ever since. No true God can be absent from most of the history of His world. The miracles recounted in the Bible are not the blueprint of the way the One True God behaves. It is no use imagining that God would give a repeat performance of the parting of the Red Sea if only we had enough faith.

The God of the Bible emerges as the God of the whole universe, creator of, involved with, and active through all nature and all history. The vital point is that the God in whom Christians believe is the one and the same God throughout and it is now that we have to seek to perceive His presence and His signs in the terms and conditions of today. We cannot be transported back in a biblical time machine and it is a denial of the God of the Bible to want to do so. The God of the Bible is a contemporary God who is working for the future. Any use of faith, Bible or Church to deny the experience of history or the discoveries of reason in the name of something detached from both and labelled 'The biblical view of the world' remains an ungodly, power-seeking and unbiblical lack of faith. It is also a denial of the fundamental Christian insight that men and women, although sinful, are 'in the image of God'. Our historical experiences and disciplined reasonings are not to be written off. They are ways in which God reveals Himself and His purposes to us.

The gift of biblical faith in the living God is to enable us to face up to reality as we discover it, or as it discovers us, not to hide away from it. Therefore any consideration of miracles has to take place within the world as we now understand it. The Bible is about how God gets in touch with, challenges and assists women and men for His glory, for Love and for their salvation and fulfilment. Miracles are signs of, and part of, this mysterious and saving interchange between God and men and women, within the world God made and continues to relate to.

For my part I am quite clear that miracles occur, but I am equally clear that I do not believe in God nor in His Son Jesus Christ because of miracles. God in Jesus is shown to be a God who acts for, through, and with His people. Because God is here today, because God is active and God is loving, and because I and all my fellow human beings are potentially open and free human beings in the image of God – there is no telling what wonderful signs and gifts are to be received in the gracious and mysterious dealings between God and women and men in His world. Only one thing is clear, God will not deny Himself to be as He has shown Himself to be in Jesus Christ. So miracles are never proofs of power, they are gifts of love to be received by faith. Furthermore, they are to be responded to in life by praising and trusting God, whether He gives us more miracles or not.

I am convinced that God is, But He is not the God of the religious or the religions but the God who is pointed to in the vulnerability and openness of Jesus. This God is a much greater mystery than we believers like to think, and the wonder of Him grows the more you contemplate it. The true God is a God of worth and hope, of struggle, offer and promise. This is the biblical God who is really at the heart of things, and is to be met with in and through everyday reality. Believers are forever projecting their limited understandings of God and falling in love with their projections as if they were the real thing. God is always being shut up by religious people who want to make Him a function of their desires instead of learning to be part of His possibilities. As many people use religion to hide from God as to get close to God.

From the very beginning, when people first came to believe that Christ was raised and alive for evermore, they came to that faith through encounters with the living Christ – not through relics or certainties or holy places or doctrines. Look at Jerusalem again – that city gives us fair warning of what happens when we get this wrong. Jerusalem – Holy City for three faiths – yet all three religions have got stuck in Old Jerusalem, stuck in past history, stuck in their old quarrels and miseries. The result makes Jerusalem a disgrace to the Lord God of the Jews, the God and Father of Our Lord Jesus Christ and to Allah. There has to be a new way forward. That, indeed, is what the Resurrection was and is about – being transformed out of our old ways and being raised to newness.

To walk through the streets of Jerusalem today, past the slogans and the military foot patrols, is to be forcibly reminded of how much that 'Holy City' needs a hope of Resurrection. Yet back in the Church of the Holy Sepulchre there is a clear sign for us. Go through the main door and stand in the vestibule. To your left is the way to the tomb, to your right is the rock of

Calvary and the memory of the crucifixion. The rock is now turned into a shrine so covered with candles and religious doo-dahs you can hardly recognise it. That is what religious people tend to do with Christ. Still, underneath it all the reality the rock symbolises remains. Unless God is mixed up in the death and the mess and muddle there is no hope of Resurrection. And in case you think that is a very gloomy note to end this chapter on, I will remind you of the punchline of the Easter story: He is not here. He is risen!

5

God is as He is in Jesus

So we are back to the question of what the Resurrection means. All Christian doctrine, worship and practice may be said to centre on this question. Doctrines, worship and practice developed for well on 2000 years lead to a good many words. We have short formulae like creeds. Then there are longer Church statements, which are supposed to define things, and now we have books upon books upon books. Can we get through to any significant simplicity now with all this weight of tradition, argument and controversy piled up all over the place?

I myself have often been told that my sentences are too involved and that I like long words too much. Many years ago I got fed up with this and decided I would put down what to me is the essence of where Christians have got to and what invites us to go on. I managed to get it down to thirteen words. Thirteen words, all of which – with the honourable exception of 'Jesus' – have only one syllable. This no doubt makes it incomprehensible. If you produce something really simple you are bound to be misunderstood – one of the rules of communication being that normally two-thirds of any sentence should be padding as people can only attend to one part in three. Be that as it may, my sentence is as follows. 'God is, He is as He is in Jesus so there is hope.' I later constructed a second sentence which supplements this (this one containing no word of more than one syllable), 'God is, He is for us, so it is worth it.'

These sentences are what I would call signposts into belief. The central point of both is that they emphasise that all faith starts from the reality of God. The question is, how do you get on to that reality? In the Christian tradition you get on to the reality of God above all through Jesus.

Here I need to make a small theological detour. The distinctive symbol of the Christian understanding of God is that of the Holy Trinity – God the Father, God the Son and God the Holy Spirit. Now this does not mean that there are three gods, there is only one God. There is a danger with the Holy Trinity that if you try to work it out too far you find yourself in a complication which either resolves itself into a celestial tea party or a cloud with three faces. This will not do. You must accept that God is a Mystery. My understanding of the Trinity goes something like this. God the Father is God who is understood to be beyond all things. He is not confined to the particular things that are going on now or to the particular ways we experience Him now or the particular knowledge we have of Him now. (Please note: throughout I am using 'He' but God is beyond gender and encompasses He/She/It; the 'He' is merely a shorthand.) So God is the Mystery behind things, the worth in things and the Mystery towards which all things are working.

Jesus is the face of God towards us; God with us and for us. So the understanding of God in the Mystery – in and beyond the world, and always sustaining the world – has to have built into it the understanding that God is so committed to His purposes of Creation, so determined to bring about His promises and so utterly involved in sustaining, that He is also to be understood as God the Son. Then there is God the Holy Spirit. Paul writes: 'Know you not that your bodies are the temple of the Holy Spirit?' The Mystery is so great and God is so fully love that He dwells in us. When we do not know how to pray (for what on earth are we to pray for, let alone what might it have to do with heaven?) Paul says the Spirit 'pleads for God's people in God's own way' (Romans 8:27, NEB). The Spirit is God within us, taking up our inarticulate groans and making them part of the whole longing, sustaining work of God. So God the transcendent Mystery of infinite purpose is one and the same God who is one with us, in and as Jesus, and this is the same God who is available within us and works through us as the Spirit. So when I say that there are three persons but one God, 'person' does not mean 'person' but there are three equally real things about the one God. Now I hope that is simple and clear, let me proceed!

In the midst of this mixed world there are signs and signals of the presence of God. The Old Testament is about people picking up signs of God and perceiving Him in their lives. As witnessed in the Scriptures a belief grows in a pattern, a presence, a promise which is involved in this world but goes far beyond it. The New Testament is about the new revelation that, in Jesus, God sent His Word – *the* clue to how we are to understand God's nature. The Gospels recount an incident when Jesus asks his disciples who they think he is, and Peter replies: 'You are the Messiah' (see, for instance, Mark 8:30). 'Messiah' means 'the anointed one' from God, in Greek 'Christos'. So the people who identified themselves with the discovery of Jesus as the Christ came to be called 'Christians'. Perfectly simple so far, but Christians through the ages have never had a very good record for living up to the power and meaning of this discovery that Jesus is to be recognised as the Christ of the Living God.

Every winter our society lavishes money and attention on the festival of Christmas. The modern celebrations have picked up so much pagan baggage and tinsel that our ways of keeping 'the Christmas story' alive can make it sound and look rather like a fairy-tale. What Christians are celebrating at the core of this festival is the down-to-earth mystery of the Incarnation – that God as Jesus spoke His last and final Word about absolutely everything. That is why there is such a fuss about the birth of this Jesus. The traditional Gospel reading for the main celebration on Christmas Day is the opening of the Gospel of John which links the person and history of Jesus with the account of the Creation at the beginning of the book of Genesis: 'In the beginning was the Word and the Word was with God, and the Word was God. And the same was in the beginning with God. All things were made by Him . . . and the Word was made flesh and dwelt among us.' The claim is that God is so really love and so truly committed to the universe which is in some real sense His creation, that He chose to locate Himself and reveal His nature in and through a particular man, Jesus, at a particular point in time and space.

Looking at the way we often seem to present the 'Christmas story' I cannot blame the secular world for its scepticism. Our celebrations of the Incarnation at Christmas tend to be highly selective. I count a total of 167 verses in Matthew and Luke which relate to the narratives of the birth of Jesus. Of these I reckon that fifty-three recount the episodes that go into the nativity plays, and form the basis for the vast majority of Christmas cards and carols. In the context of the Gospels the verses of these birth narratives do not stand on their own. They occur in a setting of twice as many verses again, and the whole collection serves as an introduction to the history of Jesus from his collaboration with John the Baptist to his death and Resurrection. Their purpose is to point forward to the fulfilment of God's purposes for the world. So long as Christians persist in embalming the message of the Incarnation in an annual ritual, the secular world can hardly be blamed for thinking that Christians deal in childish fantasies. The baby who, according to the stories, was born to live as God with us grew up to share in the miseries of human existence as well as the hopes, and gave his life for God's Kingdom that there might be a future of worth. There is no tinsel in the stories written around the birth of Jesus. We have put it there. The stories in the Gospels are about people full of faith who lived pretty tough lives yet still enjoyed a real hope because they believed in a real God.

The Resurrection declared Jesus to be the Son of God and Christians came to be convinced that in Christ God was in man, but nothing should be done to diminish the reality of the man going into uncertainty for the sake of God and God's Kingdom. The final stage of the death and Resurrection stories begins with Jesus riding into Jerusalem on a donkey (picking up a prophecy of Zechariah's about the coming of the King of Israel), people cheering, a moment of great hope – but what does it come to? Jesus was rejected, hope was crushed in crucifixion and death. The more I study the texts the more it seems to me that Jesus simply followed faithfully the way he was led. The price of suffering he paid cannot be ignored. The way Jesus followed led him to the Cross and the dreadful cry of desolation: 'My God, my God, why hast thou forsaken me?'

But what does all this mean? I can produce, because I happen to have that sort of facility, diagrams that thoroughly confuse everybody about the mystery of God, the Holy Trinity; I can talk, scarcely drawing breath, about the mystery of Jesus, but where does it come down to earth? The answer is that it comes down to earth in people. Jesus died for *us*. This is not to say that God is only met with in people or that everything met with in people is to do with God, but the thrust of the Bible is that God is interested in, and has invested Himself in, people. As the first letter of John puts it: 'If you do not love your brother whom you have seen, how can you say you love God whom you have not seen?' In short, paying attention to me, to us, and to where we are is a necessary part of being more in touch with God.

You can start on this process by looking in a mirror. Some of us need to put our glasses on, but once you are in focus gaze fairly intently and consider. When you come to think of it, is it not odd that you can think and especially that you can think about yourself? You could not think in any detail, probably, if you could not talk. You could not talk if nobody had ever talked to you. In fact, that I can think of being me depends on other people having treated me as me.

Next consider someone you know well, and love a lot. I must admit that I sometimes feel I have not got a clue as to what is going on in loved ones' heads. On the other hand my wife some-times seems to know what I am going to be thinking even before I have started the process myself. Sometimes you are right inside people and sometimes you are nowhere. There is a mystery – a mystery which sometimes contains a great deal of loneliness, sometimes encompasses a great deal of longing and yet also is sifted through with something quite marvellous. You and your loved one are just there together and you do not have to think about it at all. Look out from such a privileged position at the world and see all the dreadful things we human beings can do to each other and the mystery deepens. The mystery builds as you grow older – many of your contemporaries and friends do not just retire, they also die, and the certainty grows that I too shall die. What could be the truth about people like you and me? Is life a tragedy that comes to nothing, a piece of nonsense, or is there hope?

So many times what has served to bring me back from the brink of despair has been what I glimpse in human faces. Being human can mean being very loving, very courageous and very full of worth. It is because of what I have known through human beings that I am convinced that there must be more to life than nonsense.

I was once in New York, which can be a very depressing city, especially if you are on your own. I was doing a job with a television producer who instructed me that if I was to be an up-to-date purveyor of the Gospel I must see a list of fifteen films before I would be ready to help him produce a programme. Being at the time in an impressionable frame of mind, I set off to find the first on the list. I ended up at a late-night showing of *Easy Rider*. I know that this is what is referred to by the knowledgeable as a 'significant' film but, like many of its kind, it was also extremely depressing. I came out on to the streets of New York feeling low and rather frightened, unsettling shadows of the city's crime figures eddying in my mind. Very much alone and far from home, I set off to walk back to my hotel. By Times Square and Forty-Second Street I was thinking to myself: 'People who say that the world is hell and we are degenerate and going down the drain must be right. I am not at all sure I can believe in God.' As I proceeded glumly on my way looking back over my shoulder in case someone should decide to mug me or run me down, I heard disco music playing. As a rule I am not much impressed by disco music, but any port in a storm. I followed the sound and standing in front of this dive there were two of the ugliest people I have ever seen. One of the gifts New Yorkers seemed to have at that time was that even when they were ugly to start with they managed, by the skilful addition of unflattering spectacles and pork-pie hats, to improve on nature. It was quite amazing. So there were these two very ill-favoured people, a man and a woman, looking incredibly unattractive at first sight. They were hand in hand, dancing up and down and they were obviously immensely enjoying one another. There was a sort of glow about them, a sort of smile with their whole being. The Lord said to me: 'There, you see! Anywhere I am my image is around. People can discover me through one another, so kindly go home, go to sleep peacefully and stop being such a drip!'

The Christian claim and understanding based on Bible, Faith, Tradition and practice, is that we can take this mystery seriously. We are right to puzzle that chemicals organised into persons can think, love, suffer and hurt one another and marvel that all people need others to enable them to be people, let alone themselves. The Christian belief is that you and I are in the image of God. This is not a claim that the world is centred on men and women. We have been composed from a collection of chemicals and our bodies will decompose back into chemicals. The claim is that these ordinary elements have been fashioned into beings in the image of God able to get on to God's wavelength and respond to Him.

Signs and signals of worth and hope are all around and conviction can be renewed unexpectedly, but it is not in the nature of this world for anything to be proved beyond the shadow of a doubt. There is a struggle going on, and much in the world undoubtedly counts against God. It is foolish to pretend that it is always easy to believe that worth has an upper hand in the world. Belief in God is always challenged. There is always a question-mark about which wins – faith or nonsense. Sometimes the question-mark goes down in the same sort of desperation, despair and nonsense that Jesus faced on the Cross. Then I am reminded that the writer of the Book of Job had the same question-mark and practically swore at God. Jesus in his desperate cry on the Cross experienced the same question-mark. I find again and again that, in a very glorious and strange way, the question-mark suddenly changes into an exclamation-mark about the glory of God and the triumph of love. The hell business in life of much-loved children dying, of the sufferings of famine, bereavement, loneliness – the shouting at God – it all echoes the desolation on the Cross. In Jesus we are reminded that bang out of the middle of this despair is where the Resurrection explodes, the Holy Spirit is given and there is power to go on living and cherishing loving and worth.

In following God in the world, however convinced you are about the availability of hope and promise, you never know where you will come to. The way to coming closer to God lies through uncertainties which may make you feel that you are lost. Lostness on the way to God. Finding that you have known God but that you are no longer sure you know Him, yet still hoping to know Him again and from this supposing that you do know Him – this is very much a feature of spirituality and pilgrimage. The understanding we draw from knowledge of the Risen Christ is that it is somehow in the depths that you can be found by God and can find God.

In my time as college chaplain in Oxford I once went to see a college steward when he and I and his wife knew very well that he was dying. This man said to me after we had talked about this and that, 'Well, you don't know, sir, do you?' I replied, 'No, you don't', and we remained sitting together until I had to go home. He died two days later. Some time after, his wife rang up and said: 'I am so glad you came to see John that day because he was so cheered up when you left.' I realised then that by sitting together before the unknown in some fellowship which we shared as Christians, a third party had been present and that third party had done the trick. It would have been nonsense to say anything other than, 'We don't know' at that time. I do not even know when I say that I am convinced that we shall enjoy going on after death, how we shall enjoy or even who the 'we' shall be. But I have come to the conclusion that it really does not matter. For what I have begun to know of the God who is as He is in Jesus is sufficient assurance for me. The lively and loving relationships between God and us will produce a fulfilment which will be totally appropriate to them and an enjoyment which will be totally sufficient.

I felt this most strongly one weekend at the time of the Cuban missile crisis in the sixties when it looked as if we might all be blown up. I was struggling with this, trying to decide how to preach, when my small son came into my room to play. Looking at him I thought to myself, I know because of my relationship with him, his mother and all those I love, from what I have learnt through the Bible and how that is validated by what Jesus shows me about God, it would not be the end if the bombs went off. Life would still be infinitely worthwhile and nothing, in one sense, would be altered. The reality of love cannot be wiped away.

The Good News that evangelical Christians keep writing about on billboards in underground stations is that the universe is not too vast to have room for meaning, purpose or love. Life is not too chancey, too short, and too certainly closed by death, to be open to a future which promises fulfilment for all its best enjoyments. Suffering is not too tragic, monstrous, devastating and agonisingly destructive to be incapable of being absorbed, overcome and transformed. Men and women are not too selfish, greedy, ill-advised and capable of spoiling the good in themselves and in the world to be without the possibility of contributing to a common good which could satisfy us all. The glory which we all sometimes glimpse, the joy we all sometimes share, and longing we all sometimes have for a love which would make all things well and worthwhile for eternity, are all hints of God and what can be.

There is no answer to many of the terrible things that happen in the world. What Jesus tells us about God is that He is there with us in the suffering, teaching us to hope in the weeping and that it is the disfigured Christ on the Cross who eventually is the Christ of the Transfiguration. The point is, is God at one with the man on the Cross? Christians are convinced God is and so there is hope.

Now, what about all this talk of love? Christians, while not necessarily behaving any better than other human beings, often repeat the assertion that God is love. Apart from the normal healthy scepticism of the usual secular reaction there is a good question: what kind of love? God is not about smother love, or about the kind of love of a parent who pats errant offspring on the head with a bland 'never mind'. The way God loves has to be a definition of loving. The love Jesus demonstrated in his total obedience and commitment to God the Father and God's Kingdom, was the kind of love which risks everything – including giving everything away into suffering and death.

The Christian certainty that God raised Jesus up reshapes

fundamental assumptions if you pay attention to it. Christians have become, in a sense, so familiar with the pattern of the Gospel narratives – how they lead up to the crucifixion and then to the Resurrection, the knowledge that after Good Friday comes Easter Day – that the enormity of the shattering discovery that God raised Jesus up has been lost. The discovery that Jesus, the suffering servant, was the Messiah, the final Word of God, the ultimate clue to God's nature, reshapes the assumptions of God's power and 'triumph', posing a new definition of love which none of us have yet come to terms with.

If God is a God of Love then He is committed to freedom. You cannot be made to love. You have to learn to love. You cannot be forced to truth, you have to receive and respond to truth. You cannot be part of responding to God by a knock-down argument because that would be the work of a devil who was determined to take you out of yourself in order to change you. Whereas God is determined to enable you *to be yourself* in order that you should become the best you can be.

Love as shown through Jesus is not coercive or manipulative, it is absorbing. We all know how when we are up against something we respond with anger. Somebody fights you, you fight back; this leads to more trouble and it drags on and on. If it were possible to give the soft answer that turneth away wrath, we could be part of the way of absorbing love. A love which can suffer everything is clearly indestructible. There is the centre of hope.

Another thing about love: there is always more. It is quite clear from all the saints and much in the Bible that pilgrimage into God is a pilgrimage from something we know towards something we hope to know through things we do not know. Love is like this too. It seems to me that you discover how important love is as you begin to love, but it is only as you really fall in love that you uncover the fact that you did not know what love was. As you go on – if you go on – there are more and more demands, challenges, opportunities. One of the amazing things about growth in love is discovering how love forever stretches out in new ways, new directions.

Living by faith through Jesus Christ includes the realisation that nobody can be fully a person until other people are fully persons. I cannot be fully me until you are fully you, and that involves you being you in such a way that it enables me to be me – which involves me being me in such a way that you are enabled to be you. (Isn't it marvellous how you can confuse with words of one syllable?) In short, we are dependent on one another to be ourselves. I know from my family life and from my collaborative working life that I cannot do my job without other people. In sharing with other human beings you discover things you would never have discovered alone. There is so much more to each one of us because of being together. This, incidentally, is why Christians place such emphasis on the family. Families are not important because of something called 'morality', something stiff and unbending with clearly defined rules. The importance of families lies in relationships. People who do not have good personal relationships do not develop into good persons.

I used to have trouble with the notion of eternal life. I knew I should want eternal life because I am told that God promises it to me and, of course, it is impolite not to want what God promises. Nonetheless I could not help wondering whether going on and on would not just be an awful bore. If eternity is to involve all of us as we are then surely, as Sartre pointed out, we will truly discover that hell is other people. If being caught up into God's eternity is to be a desirable thing it must involve transformation, growth and development. A glimpse of how eternity might be infinitely worthwhile came to me when I was working for the World Council of Churches. The language problem was a continual frustration to me. How can you share communication with people who speak languages other than your own? Attending international conferences conducted in English is no solution, for English is usually a second or third language for the majority of participants. Then it occurred to me that one of the purposes of eternity might be to be enabled to learn perfectly every possible language there is so that everyone can express themselves in such a way that they will be fully understood and able to share with other people. I am comforted by this idea.

Heaven will not be a bore, for the Mystery is infinite and there will always be more to discover and to be part of.

People are that which their relationships enable them to become. If you are optimistic by nature this is a cheerful observation, but to a cynic it can be a very depressing notion. Men and women may or may not be in the image of God but I think we can all agree that they have a great facility for damaging each other. All people are liable to use the very things that make us persons in ways which spoil other people as persons.

This brings us to sin. Religious people often say that being a Christian means taking a stand and opposing sin. The question is, how do you go about this? God in Jesus has strong things to say to much of the moralistic posturing that goes on. Particularly in relation to the periodic demands that Church and Church leaders 'take a stand' on what are described as 'moral issues', but which more often than not are focused on sex (regardless of the fact that sexual sins are not the only ones nor necessarily the ones that are most damaging of persons).

To face the truth about ourselves in the light of Jesus we need to recognise that the whole business of needing to be forgiven for being a sinner starts with ourselves. Take the famous story of the woman caught in adultery (John 8:1–11). Jesus refuses to condemn her, he poses questions which remind her accusers of their own sins and he sends her on her way with forgiveness and compassion. Christians should be very cautious about people who demand the definition and condemnation of other people's sins before their own. The cases recorded in the Gospels in which Jesus is clearly condemnatory are when he is dealing with the self-righteousness of religious leaders and teachers, and exploitative traders in the Temple. Which of us can honestly face without hesitation the challenge Jesus made to the accusers of the woman taken in adultery: 'He that is without sin among you, let him cast the first stone'?

There is no doubt that Jesus is against sin, but to take a stand with Christ against sin is to take a stand with risk, promise, forgiveness and love, alongside – and indeed as one of – the sinners of the world. Yes, the God of the Bible is a God of Judgement. Creative and realistic love cannot confront sin without wrath, but this is not the wrath of a sadistic God. God judges sinners in order to save them.

Sometimes the way religious people talk about sin and confession, it sounds as if God wants us to crawl to Him so that He may graciously pick us up. It is not like that at all. As it says in the splendid Collect: 'Almighty God, unto whom all hearts are open, all desires known and from whom no secrets are hid'. God is the Truth we all, in the end, come up against. God in Jesus corrects the Old Testament view of God's wrath being terrible and annihilating, for God sent as His judge the one who sacrificed Himself for the sins of the world. 'This is love, not that we love God but that He loved us and sent His Son as an atoning sacrifice for our sins' (1 John 4:10).

The reassessment of assumptions that Jesus presents us with is that God is so much for us that we are offered the knowledge and opportunity to face our sins in a positive context. Whatever our sins, sin shall not have dominion over us (Romans 6:14). God and love will have the last word. In the eighth chapter of his letter to the Romans, Paul explains how what God was doing in Jesus was at one and the same time to judge sin 'in sinful man' and to set men and women free from sin to live according to the Spirit of God. He makes the amazing and glorious claim that this judging and saving of mankind is not just about individuals but is to do with the whole of Creation. This is no specialised divine transaction for the private salvation of a few privileged and individual souls. The God of all creation confronts what goes wrong in creation, condemns the wrong, makes the sacrifice for the atonement of that wrong in order to set us and the whole of creation free to fulfil His purposes of love and worth. This is the Gospel revealed in Jesus Christ. God judges us and calls us into question in order to make us partners in creating His Kingdom of love, justice and worth.

I have been accused of lacking a sense of sin. I would argue that I have a terrific sense of sin. It is because I know that we are all sinners dependent on the Grace of God that I am cautious about people who seek to hide behind rigid rules and regulations from their own fears and confusions about 'morality'. There is a strong tendency to turn back to the nineteenth-century belief that regulations, whether about marriage or sexual behaviour or appropriate morals, can eliminate responsibility and risk, ensuring – or at least significantly promoting – desirable behaviour. I believe this to be false. Even in morality we have to live with uncertainty. Loving and faithful morality has much more to do with having the strength to face up to reality and coping with the things that go wrong in a way which brings out worth, than with keeping religiously to certain rules and regulations.

Christians cannot solve ethical dilemmas by citing something called 'the teachings of Jesus'. Jesus was not an oracular legislator in his isolated right, nor did he lay down rules of unarguable clarity. Take the Christian debate over divorce and remarriage. There is so much invested in sex and sexual possibilities that the Christian ideal is that people should keep themselves for one sustained relationship in which both partners may grow in love over a lifetime. That is the ideal; but what are the options when a relationship fails to the extent of damaging the persons within it? Some maintain that because Jesus is recorded as saying that divorce or remarriage involve adultery, Christians are absolutely forbidden them ('Thou shalt not commit adultery' being one of the Ten Commandments recorded in the Old Testament). However, other Christians maintain that this saying of Jesus is an example of his absolute prophetic style in confronting people with the direction of the demands of the Kingdom and with their own sinfulness. It is not to be taken as legislating an invariable religious rule. This is because, the argument runs, the insights gained from the whole of Jesus's life and teachings put at least as much emphasis on forgiveness and the possibility of new beginnings as on judgement.

The teachings of Jesus always point to choices that are required in the direction of worth and against anything unworthy of God and men and women made in His image. These choices are not ritual religious choices about keeping fixed taboo-like rules, marking off Christians as belonging to a special sect of religious human beings. Rather they are open and exploratory human choices which respond to the character and purpose of God. Being a Christian is not a religious exercise. To be a Christian is to enlist in a Divine attempt to fulfil human beings and the universe. If you imagine it is a matter of keeping rules and regulations, you have not begun to understand what it is all about. (As St Paul might say; see, for instance, 1 Corinthians 15:36.)

God is out for loving all people into a relationship with Him. The Crucified Messiah makes it clear that God is for all. It is not power and self-righteousness which is the way to serve God, but love, suffering and sacrifice for the sake of worth. In the sight of God all persons have equal potential. This concept has sharp things to say to many issues that trouble our society. Paul said that in Christ there is neither Jew nor Greek, bond nor free, male nor female. This has to be worked out again and again with regard to the oppressed, to racism, to sexism and the relationship between male and female. There is a constant struggle against the boundaries built to love which we all set up around ourselves for our own comfort. The challenge of the Suffering Servant is a disturbing and questioning one for us all; but who, looking at the life of Christ, could imagine that the way of love is superficially comfortable or that worth is easily won?

All this theory comes down to earth in the shrill demands we hear in our society at the moment for the condemnation of homosexuality. This issue is specifically formulated for an Anglican bishop in the present debate in the Church about whether there should be priests who are homosexual. To me this debate provides a pressing and disturbing example of how the God who calls us to pilgrimage of faith is asking us to struggle and move on in our understanding of morality.

It is true that the few mentions there are of homosexual practices in the Scriptures are condemnatory. This is hardly surprising given the context of the society and time in which they were written. Modern advances in scientific and medical knowledge indicate that human sexuality is to be understood as distributed on a normal curve on which both the masculine/feminine distinction and the homosexual/heterosexual distinction fall in various shadings and mixtures. What was considered 'unnatural' (and therefore against God) in Old Testament times, must now be understood in the light of our discoveries about human sexuality to be part of creation. Homosexuals will always be a minority, but they are not unnatural nor in any moral or human sense abnormal. It is the shame of the Church and society that we have not yet learnt how to respond to this reality with any clarity.

I will confess that I am a product of my generation; I am not comfortable with the idea of homosexual practices. However, I know from what I have glimpsed of God through Jesus that God loves us all and wants us to be the best people we can be – that is changed but still ourselves. I also know enough about myself, and about God's open and risky way of pressing His judgements and offer of love, to be aware that when strong emotions of anger and fear are aroused, to proceed in anything approaching a godly way requires much self-reflection and sensitivity.

In the past few years homosexuals have come to be denounced and pilloried in a manner which amounts to persecution, whatever the newly active morally righteous may say. I am certain this is wrong. There is a dangerous trend which responds to uncertainties and problems in our society by looking for scapegoats among those labelled as 'abnormal' or 'minorities'. I take account of people being disturbed at the notion of practices they know little of – I share the disquiet myself in part – but I also look around at my acquaintances, past and present. I see a significant number of godly, caring and gentle persons who happen also to be homosexual. I know the ministry of many homosexual priests to have been greatly blessed; I value the friendship of many such men and their caring qualities are obvious to anyone. I am quite aware that there are homosexuals who have been convicted of abusing boys. I also know that there are many more heterosexuals who have been convicted of child abuse, rape, violence, and many other sinful and terrible things. I am quite clear that all these erring and criminal human beings are not typical of their sexual orientation.

People must come to terms with the way their feelings of fear and disquiet cloud their thinking. All Christians should be against promiscuous and destructive sexual behaviour – such behaviour is a sin against God's purposes of worth and the cherishing of persons. But I must testify that if I am called to 'take a stand' on homosexuality I hope I have the grace to stand with those persons who are attacked for their homosexuality alone – for I am certain that is where Jesus Christ would stand, with persecuted and oppressed human beings.

The Crucified Messiah upsets all our ideas of religion, chosen people and law, presenting a constant challenge to the self-righteous. There are simplicities which help us face the complexity of moral choices, but there are no plain rules and regulations which permit the cathartic hounding of transgressors. The basis of Christian life is simply trusting in the God who is as He is in Jesus, the God who is Love. Such trust is not easily acquired; it has to be struggled for with all the resources of reason, study, reflection, prayer and fellowship available to us. Some religious people claim that such trust is simple. Jesus tells us that you must be as a child if you are to come to God, they say. That is true, but there should be a clear distinction between being childish and being childlike. Being childish is to want to be blindly dependent on an authoritarian Papa or Mamma who provides every answer, however harsh, so that you may never need to take responsibility for the truth. Whereas to be as a child is to be open to the wonders and excitement of exploring the glories of God, and women and men in His image, with eyes wide open, faculties alert and leaving aside the burden of preconceptions in order simply to trust in a loving God.

In short, God is, He is as He is in Jesus so there is hope. God is, He is for us, so it is worth it.

6

God the Creative Artist

My experience and glimpse of God as the presence, power and possibility that is in things, beyond things and through things, has developed into a notion that God is an Artist. A passionate, compassionate and infinitely patient Artist. A Creator who brings into being everything that is in hope, love, risk and experiment. More than this, He risks being a collaborative Artist. He has allowed to emerge from His material beings that have their own freedom and ability to participate with Him in His work of creating the beauty and worth which will be eternal. These beings can respond to Him, but they can also disagree. This means a great deal of conflict and risk, destruction and death. For the Artist to persevere, He must be involved in His Creation up to the Cross, up to Redemption and true Resurrection – to something that will build up into an infinite achievement of worth for all eternity, a worth which is shared. This perception of the God who is as He is in Jesus, does not involve rejection of the Scriptures and biblical faith. It means going back to the Scriptures and regaining biblical faith by re-reading them in the light of where we are now.

The great medieval theologian and philosopher, Anselm, was of the opinion that once you understood what the word 'God' meant then you would be compelled to admit that God must necessarily exist. Subsequent philosophers have had little difficulty pointing out that logic cannot take you from the meaning or use of a word to the independent existence of a Being. Nonetheless many people, ever since human beings first began to articulate their thoughts, have looked at the mystery of life, love, creativity and the universe and from it intuit that there is a God.

The Christian Doctrine of God is that God is the Creator. Genesis 1 shows the Spirit of God brooding over the initial chaos and beginning to order it. God comes to be understood as the Alpha and Omega – the beginning and the end of things. A God who creates, promises and is always in conflict with the things that are against Him, His ordering and His purposes. The belief that God is always creating, sustaining and promising, was underwritten by the understanding and preaching of Jesus. If being a Christian means taking the Bible seriously as a source of revelation about what God is like and how things really are, then we are committed to the conviction that God is the reason why there is something rather than nothing.

It follows, therefore, that God is somehow or other related to everything that goes on in this 'Creation'. This means it is not possible to retire into some form of private religious cultic story about Creation – for instance, to maintain that because the Bible says the world was created in seven days then Darwin and his successors were babbling nonsense. If there is strong evidence for some form of evolution, and some time-scale of millions of millions of years in the emergence of life on earth, then we have to relate our understanding of God to this new discovery, not despite, but because of, our biblical faith in God.

People who insist that in the name of 'biblical faith' believers should deny, ignore or sidestep the results of science and human investigation are not being faithful to the biblical faith. In some sense they are atheists, for they deny that God really and truly is the Creator of all that is. Indeed, a central challenge to Christian Doctrine in the 1990s is that people must choose: Are they to believe in the God of the Bible and plunge into all the implications and complexities of modern established knowledge about the world, the universe and human beings; or will they insist on what is falsely labelled 'biblical faith' and confine God to a cultic figure shut up in old-fashioned ways of understanding the world and the self-centred notions of salvation for themselves? Either God is the Creator who can cope with everything that is, or God does not exist and Christianity is one more outmoded superstition that the world would be well shot of.

No reflective person today can be unaware of the pressures against belief in God. One such pressure is the sheer matter of scale. The problem of the vastness of the universe is not new. The Early Fathers of the Church, in their own way, had a sense of being lost in the middle of the enormity of creation and contemplated the problem of how to locate human beings within it. The solution in the Middle Ages was to turn the understanding of the universe into a clearly constructed world, centred on the known societies (based around the Mediterranean). Copernicus and his telescopes began to undermine that view but modern discoveries blow it apart. Scientists today tell us that the measurements of the universe rise at least to the size of ten to the power of twenty-four – the mathematically minded among you can work out just how many millions of millions of light years that is. Our sun is merely an average-sized star in a galaxy of hundreds of thousands of stars. Our galaxy itself is only one of some hundred thousand million that can be seen using the most powerful modern telescopes – every galaxy containing hundreds and thousands of million stars. On this scale we are diminished in ways which our imaginations can hardly envisage. Where is a Creator God to be located in such enormity?

On the other hand, just as we are scaled down in size by the immensity of the universe, we are scaled up in view of our power over our own earth. Natural calamities such as volcanoes or earthquakes can cause great havoc, and many personal tragedies, but they do not threaten life itself or the human species as a whole. It is we who do this with our activities, inventions and explorations. Our tankers spill oil that cannot be cleared up. Commercial interests combine with local poverty to burn up the Amazonian rainforests. We pollute rivers and seas and erode mountainsides. The very longing of sophisticated Westerners for 'wilderness' increasingly threatens what wilderness there is. No part of what used to be thought of as 'the vast oceans' is free from the effluents we spew out. Our industry trails dust-bowls and acid rain in its wake. Our uses of energy contribute to piercing the ozone layer and corroding other life-preserving features of our global climate, while natural resources are gobbled up apace. We dominate the earth. And yet still a very great part of the human race exists in poverty and squalor while the affluent world over-produces and consumes to excess. There is growing awareness and increasing concern about these things penetrating our societies but who knows whether the destructive spiral can be halted – is there time to preserve and prolong our future? The survival of ourselves and the eco-system on which we depend, depends on us. We have the upper hand, even if it turns out to be the sinister hand of destruction. What kind of omnipotent God of Justice and worth could allow such a state of affairs?

The immense threat which we have brought to life on earth poses urgent questions to us all as human beings, whatever our beliefs, faith or value system, but surely we who are believers and worshippers of God – whether Jew, Christian or Muslim – must now be reduced to atheists?

As if these pressures of ecology and scale were not enough, there is also the pressure of the way 'religious' people have behaved throughout history. Religious opponents have slandered one another over the years in quite blood-chilling ways. Imperial and other political powers have been organised from the earliest times to produce particular decisions in religious matters, and mobs have been mobilised (including mobs of monks) in pursuit of one opinion or another. The tones of these controversies have echoed throughout the history of mankind perhaps more than any other human concern, with fear, aggression, jealousy and suspicion. All churches and religious powers have done a good deal of harm a well as having moved in positive directions.

The picture is hardly improved in present times. We see an awful lot today of what might be called keen religion, revival or reviving religion, or even the sort of religion that is going to attract people by fitting into the spirit of the age (which is more about superficial certainties and thuggish sloganising than liberal tolerance, enquiry and openness to reality) – a spirit of having something to consume which satisfies your immediate individual concerns. It looks as though it is supposed that a living faith in God is to protect you from the realities of the world. The purpose of a belief is to endow you with certainties which somehow solve your problems to the point where they are virtually removed. Religious people, it seems, are very keen on certainties, which they claim hold absolute transcendence, while they disregard all other 'believers' who are equally certain of their different religious beliefs. 'Christian faith' is frequently seen to be evaluated, both in the media and in the claims of many exponents, by the degree of fanaticism, or fierce dogmatism about doctrine and fierce moralism about behaviour, with which it is expressed. Christians are not alone in this – the excesses of militant Islam in recent years provide a case in point. If belief in God deduced from 'holy books' really demands authoritarian defiance both of human decency and of any openness to the realities of the universe, then it is surely the plain duty of all human beings to be militant atheists.

Not only do religious people often seem unable to face reality but their beliefs can be a positive menace to the well-being of their fellow men and women. Religious 'Fundamentalism' supplies one of the most dangerous undercurrents of our age. Groups of 'convinced believers', declaring commitment to some sort of Cosmic Emperor God who desires to wipe out his enemies and calls on his followers to bully their way to sacred triumph (regardless of the fact that this regularly leaves their proclaimed aims of justice and peace trampled in their wake), do not provide a particularly convincing case for a transcendent and just God. Given the fragility of our world, any cool observer may be pardoned for imagining that such faith is more likely to lead to the human race blowing itself up, than to salvation.

So, even if God exists, and even if He made man in His image, has He not made a gigantic mistake? Surely 'god' must have vanished, leaving us alone with the knowledge that we too may vanish very soon, annihilated before our time on the biological clock because of our depredations and aggression. We are in double jeopardy. We are in immediate and unnecessary jeopardy from our careless exploitation of our environment, which has produced pollution that may choke us out of existence, while, on the other hand, our ability to blow ourselves up with our nuclear creations just might get us first. What is there for God to do but evaporate in total nonsense?

Despite all this I continue to be a believer in God. I see only one tentative, fragile and hopeful way out from under the threats to our future – that is, what if God truly is as He is in Jesus? To accept God as He is in Jesus is to accept that all forms of religious triumphalism, authoritarianism and absolutism are basically atheistic – that is, contrary to the essential nature and character of the God revealed in Jesus Christ. Taking Jesus seriously as the Word of God requires a rethinking of the notion of God's omniscience and omnipotence. If God knows everything in a computer-like way – including all the things that are going to happen – it is very difficult to believe in God at all. It certainly makes it very difficult to believe in God as in any sense loving. The God pointed to in Jesus demands that we wrestle with a new definition of omnipotence and omniscience, one which encompasses the whole concept of risk, chance and change. The concept was always present in the saints of Christianity but we have lost it in our material age. A God who chose as His Word a suffering servant must have embraced risk and forgone certainty.

Some may say at this point, how could a transcendent God forgo certainty? Surely faith in God must be about knowing for sure? The Christian tradition has never been about risk and certainty – who can start rewriting the Gospels at this late date? Why doesn't the Bishop just go and join the Green Party and leave all the real Christians to get on with their certain faith?

Let me try to 'give a reason for the hope that I have' (to paraphrase 1 Peter 3:15). The biblical texts are rich enough to allow anyone to read almost anything into them. To make any sense of the Scriptures there must be an overall pattern or direction under which the texts are to be interpreted and the core truths discerned amid the layers of story, poetry, human interpretation and barely perceived insights, in which they are conveyed. As the Greek Fathers put it: God is known to us not in Himself but through His energies. So we are called to trust God for His own sake, not for any details laid out in texts like so many magic formulae. Christians are convinced that the clue to God's pattern and direction is Jesus.

It seems to me that people do not ask themselves nearly enough what all the fuss related in the New Testament was about. It could not just have been a case of another charismatic leader who achieved the ultimate accolade of being taken after his death to be a god on earth. The Romans did this with some regularity with several emperors (though it might be argued that their hearts were not always in it).

Witness the story of aged Polycarp of Smyrna in the early part of the second century. There was, at the time in Smyrna, one of the periodic bouts of persecution against Christians with which the Romans released political steam among their citizens (nothing like a scapegoat to take your mind off political grievances). Polycarp was a respectable man of elderly years and the Roman magistrate did not want to make an example of him. He took Polycarp aside and explained he did not have to suffer, if he would only burn a pinch of incense to the emperor, everything would be fine; surely his conscience and his God would appreciate the demands of political necessity? But Polycarp replied that he had served his Lord for seventy years and he would not deny Him now. So he was put to death. He felt it more important, more real, to be faithful to the Risen Lord Jesus Christ than to temporise with Caesar, the lord emperor.

Now, the point of this gloomy little tale is that the kind of faith Polycarp, and many others like him, have been prepared to die for, is not just about 'god worship' in the sense of 'hero worship'. (My hero is bigger than yours, so I am on the winning team.) Marx argued that religion is the opium of the people. Indeed it is often used as some sort of cosmic anodyne (the world is getting too much for me: take two cosmic pills every Sunday, 11 a.m.). Real faith in God, however, is about discerning a pattern amid the chaos of the world, a pattern that promises to lead somewhere. So faith in God is about believing there is meaning to life, but more than that, it is a meaning that is leading towards some purpose and fulfilment. God's purpose, in the Christian language, is the bringing in of God's Kingdom. As I have said before, God's love is the definition of true love and we have only glimpsed the edges of it. The Kingdom is therefore beyond our imagination as yet, although I find St Augustine's description useful. This great theologian wrote that the Kingdom of God would be where men and women would so love God that they could do what they love in perfect freedom.

The energy of the New Testament accounts is focused on the understanding that the last days of the earth were rapidly approaching. People must get ready with urgency for God to make His end – the Day of the Lord when judgement will clear away all that is contrary to God's Kingdom. This urgency is reflected in the Lord's Prayer, the prayer that Jesus taught and Christians still repeat today: 'Our Father who art in heaven, thy Kingdom come'. Jesus expected God to do something decisive and final. After the crucifixion, his disciples and followers, convinced that God had raised Jesus up out of and beyond this death, recognised Jesus himself as both the sign and the means of this End which God was on the verge of bringing about. But if Jesus was God's last Word, the last word was not followed by a full stop.

This soon began to cause the early Christians problems in their evangelisation. The writer of the Second Letter of Peter referred to it in the first century of the existence of Christianity: 'First of all you must understand that in the last days scoffers will come, scoffing and following their own evil desires. They will say, "Where is this coming [in Greek, *parousia*] he promised?" Ever since our fathers everything goes on as it has since the beginning of creation.'

So Christians have a problem. The writers of our Gospel texts appear convinced that the Second Coming and the appearance of God to judge the world was at hand and that was why everybody had to believe and repent. But as time passed it looked as if they had got the message wrong. Where was it all leading? If Christians were right to expect Jesus's emphasis on the Kingdom to imply the delivery of God's promise in a dramatic and tangible form which would justify to all eyes the claims and expectations of His believers – why the delay? 'Where is this parousia he promised?'

Christians came up with various solutions. With the emergence of Constantine as the first Christian Emperor in the early fourth century some theologians began to look to the Kingdom being ushered in through the unification of the world in one Empire dedicated to the worship of the One True God. This notion appealed greatly to imperial powers and for some centuries the Church espoused versions of the theory. However, glueing God to the Church or any institution must lead most rational people to atheism. If God is the ultimate reality who is independent of, and goes beyond, all other realities, there must always be unexpectedness, openness, newness and all revelation must be incomplete. To suppose anything else is to substitute the Church or a church for God. This is clearly idolatry, whatever comforting certainties such an arrangement may produce. Guaranteed and necessary orthodoxy is not only a myth, it is also a menace.

An alternative to seeking to bring in the Kingdom via the Church or State was to continue the cliff-hanging expectation of the coming of the Apocalypse to bring an end to the miseries of life. This solution took the line that Christians have always known that we are all sinners and must expect this life to be a vale of tears. Therefore Christians are called to individual repentance in the hope of avoiding the coming wrath by gaining a place among the righteous. Some groups still follow this interpretation. It was only a few years ago that the Americans had a presidential candidate who was a firm believer in the likely imminence of the Apocalypse. He was widely reported for motivating his staff with graphic accounts, drawn from the Book of Revelation, of how the Beast would walk the earth feeding on the flesh of the damned, while the righteous chosen few would be whisked away to the sanctuary of heaven, from where they could gloat with God over the wreck of the fallen.

Surely this has to be wrong. Can we really believe that God, the Creator of this vast universe, does it all in order to save me and a few people like me? The point, value and meaning of God's existence cannot lie in His being my insurance policy or even the survival of the 144 000 or so (numbered in Revelation 7:4 following) who shall be saved. To believe such things can only support the theories of Freud and such about the projection of fears and conflicts within our selves. I believe it was Bernard Shaw who commented: 'God created man in His image and man is forever returning the doubtful compliment.'

If the obscure and disturbing Book of Revelation is really to be taken literally, and God in the End is to reveal His true nature by delivering sinners to the Beast, while sitting back in Heaven with the righteous few to watch the fun, then surely it is the duty of all decent men and women to be atheists. Such a god must be an idol, a tribal deity, a human fantasy and projection. The picture is so inconsistent with what we are shown of God through Jesus that we must have profoundly misunderstood the message.

It is important to keep our eyes on where we think God is going. So many believers seem to think that God is, so to speak, stuck up there somewhere, or fixed in the past. I cannot believe that. I am sure that God is always right here and always pressing forward. I find myself obliged to ask of much religion today – what are we so-called 'faithful' seeking? Survival of past forms of religion or service of God for the Future? For surely if God is God He dwells in His Eternity and our Future, He cannot be stuck in the past. Believers cannot use what they have formulated into religion to shut God up in. However much we may argue that the neat boxing-up is for the proper preservation of Truths – the protection of God – the fact is that our 'orthodoxies' are, more often than not, for the protection of the timidity of us would-be believers.

Being certain of our own personal hotline to the deity is not enough either. To know something because 'the Lord is in my heart' is no guarantee of anything. Before now people have found Hitler in their hearts. 'My heart' may well be telling me something quite wrong and destructive. Once again we have to keep our eyes on where it is all going. Under that perspective, a useful way to distinguish true insight from delusion is that true vision makes people more loving, more realistic, and more open – in Christian terms, more like what we know of God through Jesus.

Now, all this criticism of some tendencies in religion does not mean believing in nothing or everything in equal measure. Total assurance and total commitment are not the same as total certainty about details. The older I get, the less I am inclined to believe, but the more strongly I find I believe what I do believe. I become ever clearer on the way forward, but details about the proper furnishing of the house of faith on the way, although they are interesting, become increasingly secondary. Bishop Lightfoot once said that he was content to leave a thousand questions open providing he was convinced on two or three main points. I would agree. There are what might be termed basic ground rules to commitment to the Christian God, but they are much simpler than most of the constructions and constrictions believers and churches build up around their faith. The central facts about God seem to me to be the openness of the world to God, the love of God for us, the conviction that God is as He is in Jesus and that the Spirit of God is around to help us work out His purposes.

It is the understanding of Trinitarian faith that God is a living God and continues to unfold His purposes throughout the ages through the Holy Spirit. Some religious people seem to talk about the Holy Spirit as if He/She/It is limited to purely 'personal' work – intervening on the side of the righteous in support of their particular careers and personal ambitions. This does seem an absurd reduction of a transcendent God. The Holy Spirit as witnessed in the Scriptures is working for God's purposes for the whole of creation. He/She/It is denigrated if reduced to the level of being the originator of the impulse that leads you to comment on your neighbour's irritating habits – albeit in love and charity and for that neighbour's best interests. The Holy Spirit of the Living God is involved in every generation of believers in the continuing process of forming, testing, exploring and reforming belief, faith and understanding. So each generation of Christians contributes new insights to – takes part in new developments in – the understanding of God from the context of their times. You have to spot how God is being consistent, pick up His energies, and take it further. Believers cannot go back on what has been learnt for that 'disfulfils' the Scriptures.

Our present context and pressures link the whole of humanity as neighbours on a precious but limited planet and amplify the universal message of the Gospel. 'And this Gospel of the

Kingdom will be preached in the whole world as a testimony to all nations and then the End will come' (Matthew 24:14).Such passages can be (and frequently have been) read as demanding thuggish and desperate evangelisation – to tick off as many souls as possible from the list of mankind before an Apocalyptic end. This cannot be right if you read the message in the light of Jesus as the Word of God. Jesus behaved differently from the prophets before him. He sought sinners. He believed in the love of the neighbour, including not only outcasts but also the enemy. His love was universal. Where others sought to condemn, he emphasised repentance and forgiveness.

Once again we have to ask ourselves about our picture of God. We have a problem with 'righteousness'. The purpose of God's End is to fulfil God's purposes of justice, holiness and righteous love, but I feel we often distort the 'righteousness' with overtones of 'self-righteousness'. I do not believe that God is self-righteous. The New Testament writers often portray the acts of God's judgement as a cosmic catastrophe. The pictures are vivid and terrible but the apocalyptic strand remains stubbornly concerned with an End which is a fulfilment of, and in continuity with, creation and the response of men and women within creation. 'In keeping with His promise we are looking forward to a new heaven and a new earth, the home of the righteous' (2 Peter 3). Even in the much-quoted Book of Revelation, the vision of the New Jerusalem (Chapters 21 and 22) is a universal vision. This is not a cultic god selecting a chosen few to join with the angels in a heavenly rapture. (It seems to me one of our problems is the limitation of human imagination when it comes to heaven. We have so much more to draw on to colour our depictions of hell, but our visions of heaven do tend to be rather sketchy.)

To pursue a triumphalistic picture of God, one which relies on God to come in like a wrathful Father to clear up the mess made by sinful man, is to be led up a blind alley which may well trap humankind into destroying itself. Such faith is not taking account of the risk God takes – the creativity, the love of God. Adherence to the ways of God known through Jesus, means that followers cannot demand certainties or absolute answers. Faith must be a question of making responses to a living God. The existence of God does offer the possibility of individuals getting on to real truth, but it is not the sort of truth that can be plucked out of a book, banged into the head and then possessed forever. The possibility is of being taken up by a truth, a truthful way of living, which will draw the faithful ever further into the unknown Mystery.

Nevertheless, can even the Greatest Mystery cope with the contradiction of God by human beings, and the diminution of human beings by the universe? I am clear that there can only be a personal answer to this. The clue must lie in the fact that it is we who are aware of the scales by which we measure the enormity of Creation. We have even, in some sense, invented them – though in a sense which reverberates with the notion that we have discovered them. For these human beings, insignificant little blobs of matter in the vastness of the universe, turn out to be able to think. We can not only think about the mud from which we came, and ourselves, but also chart the universe from the millions of stars in the galaxies around us to the most minuscule scales, such as a millionth of a millionth of an inch, dealt with in quantum mechanics. The baffling complexity of it all underlines the vastness and depth with which we, and faith with us, must live if we are to face up to where we now stand as human beings. But the mystery remains – what is the universe doing in this thinking, feeling and wondering about itself? – for however brief a period and in however small a corner. Perhaps it is because, in however hidden, mysterious, struggling and fragile a way, there is 'something personal' about it. Indeed we are the clear evidence that there is something personal about it. Men and women are part of some very great mystery and it may very well be that in some basically true and real sense they are in the image of God.

If we have a personal relationship to God, there is the opportunity of being in touch with eternity and everything in a moment. We may have limited time but this time is of singular importance, and we should be concerned with making the best possible use of the moment, the best possible use of the world and the best possible response to our neighbours right now.

Under the pressures and threats of our present times we know that it is not a question of what each of us as individuals does individually and religiously between this moment and our individual deaths. We are indeed 'all bound up in one bundle of life'. Under the threats to our one world our neighbours extend across the whole earth. In the Christian understanding, God's final Word was expressed in a particular, historical, flesh and blood, man crucified. In Jesus of Nazareth, who 'suffered under Pontius Pilate', God affirmed these very temporary persons within the context of a universe of whatever scale. So all persons have value and a role at this particular time – even in the face of threats so great that they raise the question whether for us the Future has a future.

We have to encompass an understanding of the element of risk in faith. If God is the Creator, then He has taken on risk in creation – so much so that He must live with uncertainty on an eternal scale. Jesus as Lord makes it clear that God is the God who risks Himself because He is in very truth, and through all eternity, the God who is Love. God has risked being limited by His own creation – by giving the men and women created in His image freedom. God has so risked Himself that much of the world ignores Him, denies, contradicts Him. Atheism at many times for many people seems far more logical and likely than faith. Especially when you consider how proponents of God so often express their faith through fear, their zeal in persecution, and their so-called commitment to God in refusals to face reality. But God is not diverted by the effects of the risks He has taken, for He is Love and Divine Love cannot be diverted, defeated nor deflected from the pursuit of creation, salvation and fulfilment.

If God takes risks, how can his followers expect to avoid them? And why should we want to, for 'we are not among those who shrink back and are lost; we have the faith to make life our own' (Hebrews 10:39). 'Here we do not have an abiding city, but we are looking for the city that is to come' (Hebrews 13:14).

God took the risk of being limited by His own creation – by making men and women in His image and giving them freedom. Jesus, in being the man God chose to become, might mean that

God has risked His creation and needs to be involved in it in order to bring about His purposes of love and worth – not only for our sake but for His. God is not quite as detached and able to do things just for our sakes, and not His, as we might like to think. If He is Love, God might have got Himself rather over-involved. If God has expressed His commitment to the logic of what He has done by getting mixed up in, indeed identified with, the particularities of this process, all the questions will always remain. Was Jesus God with us or is it just a set of stories? Was Jesus's life on earth an enterprise of failure marked with the finality of death, or a proclamation and promise opened up by the reality of his Resurrection and therefore a promise for all resurrections? It seems to me the question-marks will always remain until the End.

So what difference can such a God make to the modern world – to the terrible possibility of nuclear destruction, say? God as He is in Jesus provides the certainty that such destruction need not happen. Quite possibly there is no future, but this need not be so. The political leaders of our globe do not have the last word about anything, never have had and need never have. This is the message of biblical books like Daniel or the Apocalypse, quite as much as the simple message of a simple faith in God in His mystery and love. Every effort at a wider, more generous and more hopeful view of the world, like every urgent action and struggle for peace, has its chance. No chain of events need reach its apparently inevitable end until midnight has struck. Under God we always live at five minutes to midnight. Urgency is demanded but fatalism and hopelessness are forbidden.

God as He is in Jesus is the ultimate source of the resources by which, in a multitude of ways, distrust, narrow self-interest and self-centred incompetence can be challenged and worked against while neighbourliness is developed. It is amazing how men and women can and will rally for helping one another, for facing disaster, for developing new ways of coping with problems and possibilities. The fire of creative love, the insights of our need for one another, and the visions of a better world and more co-operative societies are never quenched. This is so because God is not ready to be defeated and we who are in His image sometimes and sufficiently know this.

Of course it is easy to despair at the sheer size and scale of human problems. I was once travelling by train across Java for the World Council of Churches. As I was jolted along I suffered a wave of claustrophobia. There were some 120 000 000 people trapped in the sunshine and bright light of that tropical island. One hundred and twenty million people, most of them so poor that they lived forever on the verge of starvation. It seemed that nothing could be done. Then the Lord, or maybe just something I had read in a book, said to me: 'Of course nothing can be done if you think of these 120 000 000 people as 120 000 000 problems. But if you can help them to think of themselves as 120 000 000 resources there is no telling what you can do.'

I admit that I do begin to think at times that God has taken too great a risk. But as I believe in God who is as down-to-earth as Jesus, I must not allow myself to think it is an impossible task. Because of Jesus, because of what I have learnt through friends and family about love, I accept that it is not up to me to live with all the evils of the world. That is what God in Jesus has taken on. It is up to me to keep hope alive in myself. You can never cease wrestling with the balance between the risk God has taken, the responsibility we have, and the mystery that lies in between.

In the midst of the risks, however, men and women in the image of God cannot dodge the issue of responsibility. We cannot kid ourselves that by refusing to be responsible we will always be given infinite chances. We have to take responsibility seriously just as we have to take freedom seriously. This is not to say that only those who have been told about God and respond to Him are saved. If God is Love we can rely on Him to cope with the inequalities of opportunity among human beings. Believing in the sort of God who raised Jesus up, as I do, I believe that there is a realm which is God's into which we may pass after death. We are part of a much bigger plan than just this brief existence. But I cannot convince myself that we automatically pass into God's realm. I do not believe in Hell but I do believe that, as we are responsible beings, if you have a chance to love, to respond to the energies of God, then you must move in that direction. If you persist in moving in the opposite direction then you may do yourself out of a life and come to nothing at death.

God as He is in Jesus is the Mystery who is beyond whatever happens, as well as the Mystery totally committed to, and risking Himself in and through, whatever happens. I cannot say I know at all clearly what this means or will mean. Only that I cannot believe that if we turn our back on God that will destroy God. What we must face is that if we totally turn our back on God, it will destroy us. But the 'quite possibly' need not happen and we have to respond so that it will not happen.

I am quite aware that, like Anselm's circular argument that once you understand what God means you must of necessity believe in Him, all this may well seem arguments of narrow interest to a few 'religiously minded' folk. When it comes down to it I can only really testify that as I grow older I have the increasing sense of being part of something great, glorious and gracious – although at the same time something very bewildering and occasionally threatening. We ought to be terrified by the abuse of our powers, but I am convinced that this very terror is being put upon us by God in His loving purposes that we may be led to repent individually and collectively. Infinitesimal specks though we are in the vastness of the universe, we are persons who can love, respond, and are free to share in the great mystery of God's creation and promise.

Perhaps this sounds all too far-fetched for sober men and women facing the twenty-first century. But given our dawning understanding of the danger we are to ourselves – dangers symbolised in the ecological pressures caused by our exploitation of our environment – I wonder whether even the most sceptical cannot glimpse the force of 'Except ye repent, ye will all likewise perish', and can avoid pausing, however briefly, to wonder about the meaning of life.

7

'Interfering in Politics'

It is always something of a surprise to me that people should even think of asking, 'Why should the Church be concerned with politics?' I have to admit that when faced with this question, the unworthy thought that generally crosses my mind is 'Oh dear – where to start? – I can't be explaining very well; you just don't understand about God, love, creation, responsibility and neighbourliness.' But then, that is *my* failure, so I shall try to give a coherent account of my understanding of the Church's contribution to the State.

All those who want the Church to keep out of politics have yet to make the case as to how this can be reconciled with the Gospel, for politics affect the way people live, affect issues of neighbourliness, affect the whole question of the very sustainability of life on earth. If you are going to believe in a real God who copes with the whole of reality, then you have got to be concerned with more than just what goes on in your own individual heart. You have to be concerned also with what goes on in society, for society shapes us all. Society can enable us to be indifferent to terrible things, or create the conditions under which we can stand up together against injustices and try to change them.

Put simply, it is the role of Christians in society to insist again and again on the priority of persons – to be ready to stand up, even when we lack the physical resources, for treating all people as they should be treated – that is, as persons of worth. If this calling is to have any real substance it will bring those who follow it into areas which some may call 'political'.

The Bible has always raised questions to society through its prophets and ministers about what is happening to the poor and excluded. Biblical authority for being concerned about social justice follows from the theme in the Old Testament of how a society is to be judged by the way it deals with the people who get left out. In Isaiah, for instance, you find the prophet (on behalf of the Lord) blasting away at social injustice in no uncertain terms.

> Shame on you, you who make unjust laws and publish
>   burdensome decrees
> Depriving the poor of justice
> Robbing the weakest of my people of their rights,
> Despoiling the widow and plundering the orphan.
> What will you do when called to account
> When ruin from afar confronts you?
>
> (Isaiah, Chapter 10)

There runs through the Old Testament (not least in the Psalms) the ever-growing and unshakable conviction that there is a moral power and possibility buried deep in, and at work in, the often savage randomness of human affairs. The prophets and psalmists alike, despite some pretty dreadful experiences, saw a pattern in life that made it more than just survival of the fittest. They perceived and doggedly hung onto evidence that in the midst of natural disasters and man-made oppressions it was still possible, and indeed right, to believe in and respond to a God of justice and love.

Take Jeremiah. Page after page of doom and gloom but in the midst there is the Lord. The seas rage mightily, the heavens do this and that, and the sun runs all over the place, but then you come to the Lord and the Law and then you come to the people. The point is made again and again that the Lord is the ultimate overriding power and that He is concerned to bring men and women to His ways of justice, love and peace. As a very part of this concern, the Scriptures tell of the Lord's anger against all the deceitful and distorting ways of men. This anger is not a matter of God throwing a tantrum, an outburst of peevishness at the disobedience of men and women. It is a burning anger and outrage which is all of a piece with the longing for holiness and righteousness. This anger is crystallised in two ways: opposition to idolatry and concern with the treatment of the outcasts of society.

The Old Testament writers were clear that the flourishing of societies was related to the communal standards of justice and morality maintained by their individual members. In short, morality and godly behaviour are to be linked to social justice. The question is how this principle should affect the behaviour of individual believers.

Take the saying of Micah in the Old Testament: 'God has told you what is good, and what is it that the Lord asks of you? Only to act justly, to love loyalty, to walk wisely before your God' (Micah 6:8). That looks pretty straightforward, but what does it actually mean in everyday life? We could say it is a personal code. I am to act justly. Presumably that assumes I know what is unjust. I may refer to the Ten Commandments on that score. However, there have been some pretty extreme views of justice developed among mankind. Some consider it just, in certain cases, to execute and mutilate people for misdemeanours considered to be offensive to God. To love loyalty. Presumably it was loyalty to a Party and Idea exalted above conscience, that led so many Nazis and Stalinists to collaborate in the massacre of hundreds of thousands of fellow human beings in purges and death camps. To walk wisely. It could be said that if I and my people have the chance of setting up a wondrous and utopian state if only these few thousand anarchists and agitators could be done away with, it might be wise, for the good of the majority, to so do away with them.

Once again what looks simple at first becomes distinctly complicated in application – particularly if you are intent on hanging the worship of God on the keeping of a certain code of personal morals.

It is the Christian insight that Jesus, as the Word of God, focuses and draws together the potentially confusing elements in the Bible into a new perspective. Jesus reaffirmed the Ten

Commandments, but when asked what the core of the Faith was, answered: 'Thou shalt love the Lord thy God with all thy heart, and with all thy soul and with all thy mind. This is the first and great commandment. And the second is like unto it, thou shalt love thy neighbour as thy self. On these two commandments hang all the law and the prophets' (Matthew 22:37–40).

The love of God, according to Jesus, is to be pursued through the love of the neighbour. All other Commandments and injunctions are to be focused around this twofold love of God and of the neighbour.

The question then arises – how are we supposed to balance all these other elements around this great focusing love? We all sin, but some of us are particularly unlovely in our sin. How are we to stand up against the sinfulness while loving the individual? A favourite charge of tabloid leader writers against Church leaders is that they are altogether too wishy-washy about sin. (In view of the material to be found in many of their papers, certain of our journalists do show interesting signs of longing for the hell and thunder preachers of yore – perhaps they have something on their consciences?) How are we to combine the love of the neighbour with wrath against sin?

One neat solution proposed to this puzzle of just how we are supposed to love our more anti-social and unattractive neighbours, is that we do not exactly love ourselves when we fall below our own standards. So it is right to chastise and marginalise sinners into repentance – the worse the transgression, the harsher the punishment and alienation. This should be for the good of the soul of the transgressor as well as for its other social uses (such as retribution, dissuasion and social revenge).

However, this does not quite fit in with what Jesus taught. He put emphasis on forgiveness as well as personal responsibility for repentance. He preached that God's love was for all, but especially for all sinners. God, according to Jesus, is out to love all sinners into repentance and conversion, not to constrain them into it through dogmatic piety.

When Jesus was asked to elaborate on how you were supposed to follow the second Commandment of loving the neighbour, he did not give a list of appropriate moral behaviour, he told a parable. The parable was the tale of the Good Samaritan who helped the man beaten by robbers and left for dead by the road that ran through the pitiless and barren wastes of the Wilderness (Luke 10:25–37). In this story the neighbour was the 'one who had mercy' on the man who was in need. That neighbour was an unexpected and irreligious individual. He was not the Levite, who was the religious man, nor the Jew, who was the accepted man. It was the Samaritan, the outsider, who did the right thing.

This story represents a significant shift of focus from the concerns of the Old Testament writers. Personal responsibility remains, but the individual's behaviour is certainly not assessed by piety or the keeping of religious rules. The Levite, the religious man, passed on the other side of the road rather than help the man in need. In this teaching of Jesus, the challenge is to us all to live out the love of God through the love of the neighbour in a way that goes far beyond a religious obsession with individual 'sin'. The love of God is opened up to the whole realm of experience in the charge to 'have mercy' on those in need.

People matter because they are persons and their individual selves. In Christianity this fact is celebrated at Baptism, a ceremony at which you are given your name in the name of the Trinity. This to indicate that you are meant to be you and that it is part of the purpose of the eternal, holy and universal God that you are meant to be you as you. I am particularly touched by the way one Greek Orthodox theologian expresses this – he says that God the Father has a sort of personal name which is Father; God the Son has a personal name, Jesus; and the Holy Spirit does not have a personal name because it is all our names.

All individual persons are of worth, and individualism may indeed be at the heart of the Christian understanding of things, but this does not mean that the individual is a solitary unit independent of community. It has become fashionable lately to contend that the essence of Christianity is choice. This is a perversion. The essence of Christianity is love for the neighbour and love of God. It is through the pursuit of these loves that you become the sort of person, by God's Grace, whose choices can be trusted. The choice comes later. You have to be set free from

the sort of person you are, in order to make the sort of choices
that would actually help other people and so please God. St
Augustine said, 'Love God, and what you like, do' – but you
have to be changed first by your love of God or your choices are
as likely to do harm as good.

The challenge to love your neighbour as yourself is not a
comfortable one. It is a profoundly disturbing charge which
demands, in theological language, repentance and conversion.
That is re-thinking, and from that re-thinking a re-building of
the self with a consequent change of attitude and action.

Another implication of Jesus's teaching is that paying attention to justice and 'having mercy' on those in need is not a
matter of charity. It is a matter of individual and communal,
spiritual and material flourishing. If we are all bound up
together in one life – if none of us can be our best selves (as we
are intended to be as creatures made in God's image) until we
are *all* enabled to be our best selves – then there can be no moral
superiority about paying attention to those in need. Nor can
social justice be a luxury to be aspired to only 'when we can
afford it'. The Christian insight is that no society which hopes to
flourish can afford not to pay attention to social justice. In short,
the charge to love your neighbour as yourself relates to some
basic and commonsense things about the disciplines and
opportunities of living together.

However, many Christians, particularly Christian politicians, have their doubts about the involvement of bishops in
social concerns. They like belonging to a nominally 'Christian
society' but feel that the contribution of that faith to that society
should be kept to the level of concern with the personal behaviour of individuals. As one Government minister put it, in a
debate in the House of Commons in the 1980s, 'Spiritual guidance should in the end remain of far greater importance to any
Church leader of whatever faith than any question of how to
divide the national cake. In the absence of some sort of priestly
theocracy running this country, such decisions remain a matter
for the elected government and Parliament to decide, and in the
end for no one else.'

Quite so. But if spiritual guidance is effective it will affect the material. Personal piety is not enough for God. The spiritual is supposed to change the attitude of the outward, material man (I can imagine that the Levite of Jesus's story might well have considered himself an expert on 'spiritual guidance'). It is all too easy to be in favour of the Church so long as its preaching reinforces existing social assumptions and restricts its efforts to the individual spiritual comfort of individual believers. The truth is that Christianity is indeed a deeply spiritual religion but it is also a faith which lays considerable emphasis on discovering the love of God through the community. The One True God is a God of justice and love. Justice and love have no meaning if they are only applied to the self – they are concepts which require application in a community.

The role of the bishop in society is certainly not to aspire to replace the elected government, but neither is it confined to rearranging the internal spiritual furnishings of the faithful. It is twofold: firstly to remind individual believers that their faith is supposed to make a difference, and secondly to remind society that social health is related to social justice and it is to the advantage of us all to pay attention to the priority of people above theories, expediency or the selfish interests of powerful groups.

It is easy to forget what a sharp story the tale of the Good Samaritan is. Jesus was asking a disturbing question – a Wilderness question – about who is my neighbour? Who is getting left out, being badly treated, feeling neglected, and why?

Going around my diocese I am particularly challenged by this question. Because of the way things developed in the North, the rise of heavy industry in the last century and the more recent decline of our country's manufacturing base, the North East is particularly a place where developments have left pockets of people marginalised by society. I have come to identify these groups as the forced out, the dropped out and the people who are left out. The forced out are all the people who have been made redundant because of the collapse of manufacturing industry and find themselves left unwanted. The dropped out are the young people who know even before they leave school that, in some areas, only one in eight of them has the chance of a job. So why should they try to fit into society? Then there are the real left outs. The people who have become concentrated in our poor estates and who, whatever the intentions of the Government or anyone else, are being more and more badly treated by the present developments in the welfare system.

It is my perception that our society seems to be building up the numbers of people whom no one will recognise as 'neighbour'. People without hope, with no sense of belonging, no status; people who are simply left by the wayside.

It is not to be wondered at that many people find this irritating. We all like to feel we are part of a prospering country and all is going well (particularly if we ourselves are doing well). It is unpleasant to be reminded of things we may well feel we can do nothing about. Bishops have no right raising questions without suggesting answers, and furthermore, they should not dictate to elected governments on matters, the complexities of which they know nothing about.

Belief in a transcendent God who is greater than anything, means that you have always to question your own and your government's understanding of things. Loving the neighbour in practice means having your ways of seeing things and doing things constantly challenged and expanded. It involves rising above your own views of your own affairs and trying to pay attention to the experience of other men and women, other neighbours.

Christian churches are particularly well placed to find out what is happening to neighbours up and down the land. Bishops do not just drop in on comfortable congregations on official visits. They head a team of priests, deacons and lay-workers who work alongside people of all sorts and all conditions on an everyday basis. This is the true bedrock of experience which a bishop is able to draw on. In addition to the parish-based ministry there are sector ministers working in specialised fields: industrial chaplains in factories and enterprises, education officers working in schools, prison chaplains in the prison service and hospital chaplains in the NHS. The Church of England, in common with other churches, has both diocesan and national Boards of Social Responsibility and Education; teams of people who co-ordinate experience, collate detailed reports and statistics, and collaborate with a wide range of secular organisations. In short, the churches are neither unrealistic nor ill-informed. In many ways bishops could argue that they have more to do with ordinary people than most politicians – particularly national politicians who, by the nature of their jobs, have to spend a large proportion of their time in the rarefied company of the politically active. It is the experience of this network of people, and especially the people in the parishes of my diocese, which form the central resource from which I draw the material for all my sermons and reported remarks.

So bishops are in a privileged position. We get around rather more than most, meet a wide variety of people and head up a diverse and informed group of people who work in a wide variety of situations. In this privileged position we can come across things that are, according to common public perception, not supposed to exist.

In the first year of my episcopacy I found myself flung into the headlines for a speech I made in the regular November meeting of my church's General Synod. The occasion was a debate on a report entitled *Perspectives on Economics* prepared by the Anglican Board of Social Responsibility. In my speech I referred to the case of a family in my diocese who did not have proper shoes for their two boys with the result that the children had to wear the one pair on alternate days. This story was immediately lampooned in the press. The Bishop was either foolishly gullible to have swallowed such a tale – let alone to have repeated it – or was mischievous and trying to mislead. Either way, neither was exactly a flattering opinion to draw upon oneself. Nevertheless I still stand by that speech.

The case I referred to had been part of a briefing (containing several instances of cases involving similar poverty) given me by a group of advice workers operating in a Community Centre in a particularly poor area of my diocese. I trusted and knew the people who gave me the cases. Subsequent information and letters sent to me confirmed that, indeed, there were plenty of families who were so poor they were having to apply to charitable funds for shoes for their children. The 1984 miners' strike was in its depths at the time and existing hardship was being exacerbated.

Apart from highlighting an instance of the real poverty being tucked away in our society, my reason for raising the case had been to focus attention on the Social Security reforms that were being prepared at the time. One of the features of these reforms was to prune down the number of instances where emergency payments would be made. Under the existing system it was already very difficult to claim assistance from the DHSS to buy clothing, however dire the need. Once the reforms were brought in, it became more or less impossible. The general belief was – and largely continues to be – that the level of poverty which generates the need for such payments does not exist in our country. The evidence being presented to me was that it does. While the press was running colourful tirades against 'social security scroungers', the Mayor's Fund in Sunderland (a charitable trust specialising in providing children's shoes in cases of extreme need) dealt with over 5200 individual claims in one year.

At least the publicity led to the Granada Television *World in Action* team bringing the Minister up to Sunderland to make a programme on the proposed reforms. So the coverage did lead to a brief highlighting of the issues. However, the national press was not in a mind to be converted. When some of our local papers chose a journalist to be taken around by advice workers to interview families on the books and test the existence of hardship, some thoughtful articles ensued. (They agreed that, to minimise the intrusion into vulnerable people's lives, the papers would elect one journalist to represent them all.) The national papers, on the other hand, immediately dropped the story.

This experience highlights what is involved in taking a stand as a Christian. Pursuing faith can lead believers to find themselves standing in a place which is outside, and perhaps in conflict with, those stands expected or demanded by the various local establishments. It can lead you to stand up in ways which often disturb and are threatening to those who want security. You can find yourself posing awkward and unwelcome questions to what is normally taken for granted as the very basis of running states, or communities or churches. It is at times useful, and oddly comforting, to remember that our Saviour himself was not always widely popular. Indeed, he was felt to be so irritating by the Roman civil authorities and the Jewish religious authorities that they had him crucified. Christians must never forget what kind of Saviour they attempt to follow.

If you are committed to a God of justice, truth and love then you have to stand up and witness to what you see – however troubling or uncomfortable that might be. This is one of the gifts that Christians can bring to society. When a politician argues a case, you always have to keep in mind that he or she is arguing to prove a particular political point. He or she has plumped for one set of facts – selected for quite often perfectly good reasons – and argues with professional conviction that these are the most important facts. However, there are always 'facts' that people prefer to ignore. At the time of the 'pair of shoes' story the Government aim was to reorganise an inefficient and inadequate benefit system. Many of their criticisms were perfectly good. The system was indeed cumbersome and inadequate to people's needs. However, at the same time another perfectly good set of facts were being ignored – even denied. These included the fact that there was a considerable number of people who were in real poverty in areas of high unemployment who were going to be made worse off by the proposed reforms.

As a Christian witness to this process, the only response can be persistent attempts to make the reality of such people's lives plain so that we can all recognise it. This must not be done in anger but in analysis and a steady laying out of the ignored facts. This is what I have always attempted to do.

One of the most challenging human questions is: how do we 'have mercy' on neighbours who are not just individuals who have fallen into a ditch after having been attacked by robbers, but the thousands upon thousands of people who are 'in the ditch' marginalised by society?

We now have clear evidence that a serious and substantial contribution to the fate and suffering of neighbours is made by structures and trends in economics and the organisation of society. Concern with neighbours must lead beyond private charity to questioning the causes which marginalise some people in our society. Why are people poor, left out, unable to cope? Paying attention to the factors which oppress people is not just a political question, it is a human and a godly question.

It is the business of the Church to be part of pressing the urgent justice and human questions and to get people to face them. The Church is not there to dictate answers. It is perfectly true that priestly theocracies are no better at running states than secular governments. (If politicians sin politically then religious people sin religiously.) However, it is the role of the Church to remind those in power that none of us can claim to have absolute answers; there is always the risk of being wrong. This is as much true for the politicians and the policies they pursue as for the Church and its concerns.

That's all very well, I can hear the politicians say, but the Bishop of Durham got into trouble because he did not follow his own rules. He went out campaigning on particular issues. This was divisive and definitely unfair. As some slightly ponderous wit wrote in *The Times* in 1984: 'Bishops who wish to have their say on public issues of the day and for a party draw their swords can do so in the House of Lords. Is it not extremely odd to do so in the house of God?' So, bishops may raise issues of social concern but they should not, for instance, comment on a miners' strike from the pulpit or discuss elections in a sermon. Once political words are spoken from the pulpit, the word of God is sullied and the pastor who alienates some of his flock on political grounds abandons his primary pastoral duty. (Never mind if the words of God are pressed into the service of politics, that is another matter. More of that later.)

I am clear that every one of my sermons in the House of God have been, and will always be, concerned with the fact that because God is a compassionate lover of people, a bishop must raise questions about particular policies which seem to be pushing some people to one side. That is part of the job of a bishop whatever the political complexion of the government in office. The point about Jesus is that in him God took the risk of coming down to earth and getting mixed up in the ordinary affairs of men and women. We – all those who claim to follow him – have to take the same risk. I do not claim to be right. I only say that there are questions which must be faced if our belief in God as He is in Jesus is real.

Take the example of my Enthronement Sermon which first brought me the tag of 'troublesome priest'. I preached that sermon in the midst of the 1984 miners' strike. In one corner of my diocese the majority of employed men were at that time miners (many pits have closed since then). So a large section of the local population was either directly involved in the strike or was associated with it. Whatever the rights and wrongs of it, the strike was splitting the society I was supposed to serve. Police were being put in impossible situations, communities were split and many families were being made miserable. The conflict was damaging society and damaging neighbours. The Church is out, in the name of God, to build up society and care for neighbours and I chose to preach on 'The Cost of Hope'. Two-thirds of my text went unremarked by the press. It was too theological. However, as I believe theology is relevant to real life I also applied mine to the situation at hand. In the name of God I was challenging any dogmatism in politics which is pushed too far in an inhuman and impractical direction. At that juncture the miners' leader, Arthur Scargill, and the chairman of the Coal Board, Ian McGregor, were both aggressively entrenched in transparently extreme positions. My theme was that the cost of hope involved both sides backing down from their intransigent positions. My perception was that the health of the community required a compromise.

My struggling attempt to be specific and not generally speaking and bland was taken as an outrageous interference in politics. I was represented by the press and the party of Government as siding with the miners. Many miners felt I had sided with the Establishment. I felt I had tried to side with the community.

I have never regretted any of the risks I have taken in speaking out from my faith. That is not to say that I rejoice in annoying those fellow Christians who disagree with me. However, I believe it is a misconception to expect all Christians to agree, either between themselves or with their leaders. I am called to be an apostolic bishop in the Church of Christ. A bishop is supposed to point to a hope of the worth and glory and graciousness of God and then draw out implications that follow from this knowledge of God. I try to be everybody's bishop in the way I treat individual persons and groups of persons as having their right to their own intentions and perceptions. I am arguing about policies, likely effects and ignored facts. Jesus died for sinners; we are all sinners and he certainly died as much for Tory sinners as Labour sinners or politically indifferent sinners. It is a central truth that no one can be written out of being a Church member or a Christian because of wrongdoing – if that were the case then no one would qualify as a Church member or a Christian. However, if the desire to avoid dividing people reduces expressions of faith in the One True God, the Creator, who so loved men and women that He made them in His image, to mere 'comfortable words', then division must be risked. We are, after all, talking about Faith and a conviction here that is supposed to mean something. If it does, then it cannot be denied.

In reply to the charge that in risking being divisive I, or other Christian leaders who raise social questions, are damaging our cause by emptying the pews, I would respond emphatically. I firmly believe that there is a very close connection between finding realistic and effective ways of bringing signs of love to neighbours who are trapped in their thousands – and who are trapped far more by social structures than individual sins – and regaining our power to preach the Gospel with effectiveness in and to society.

The question is not just one of social justice. It is also a matter of the health of the religion itself. The Scriptures contain dire warnings about what happens to communities when religious rules and rituals become the only expression of a religion socially observed, so that the religion in practice ceases to reach out either into the living reality of God or the living practices of society at large. The great prophets, Isaiah, Jeremiah and Ezekiel, all denounce such behaviour as turning away from God. According to them, it was because the peoples of Israel and Judah had fallen into this habit with the worship of false gods (idols) and because their kings and courtiers pursued exploitation and injustice (they did not look after their neighbours), that catastrophe overcame them.

The warning is twofold, both to the Church and to the State. As is often the case, the observation of the prophets is a severely practical one. They pointed out that the treatment of the poor and the standards of justice in a society are a particular way of measuring its stability and viability. But their strictures also warn against turning religion into private assemblies existing solely for the self-selected spiritual benefits of their members. Christians are not called to recruit to 'our' faith. They are sent to serve God's Truth and Praise in this world that they might be part of God's transformation of this world.

Many people say in a vague sort of way that somehow or other they believe in some sort of God but they do not find religious talk or the behaviour of many of the religious in any way credible or engaging. In response, it is no use simply mouthing words of comfort or simply saying that people matter. It is even less use saying that God makes it clear that people matter. Dragging the word 'god' into things gets us absolutely nowhere unless Christians so live out of their understanding of God that they become the sort of people who, by what they are and what they do, are living indications that people matter, and that God makes a living difference to how, why and where people matter.

So Christians are called to develop their discipleship in social and communal ways. You cannot communicate God to people, or receive the reality of God from and through people, unless you are 'in communion' with them. It is a matter of what the New Testament calls 'Koinonia', which means having things in common. If we have nothing in common with people who suffer from the way we organise our society then we cannot 'communi-cate' with them. Unless believers in God can show other people that what matters to them in their individual lives and hopes and despairs matters to God, and therefore to His believers, then there is no hope of communicating the Gospel. The challenge to Christians is so to serve, to be so involved in the things that really matter to people, that they can be part of getting over the message of the reality of God, of Love and of the Resurrection. This service also involves paying attention to structures and how the way we organise our society affects our neighbours.

Let me give an example. A vicar in my diocese takes me to see a day-care mother-and-toddler group on a particularly run-down estate. Some extremely tough and resilient local mothers are in this effort presenting a shining glimmer of hope and neighbourliness in a very depressing situation. A key figure in the project is a lady who lives in a small house with five grown-up children. There is very little money, and jobs in the area are very scarce, yet somehow they survive with an element of cheerfulness and mutual support. Then the Poll Tax is imposed. A rational look at the situation convinces me that the money to pay the bill – even though it be but 20 per cent of the full rate – for six adults does not exist and this family is hit by another devastating blow. It is alleged that if they are in real need people can recoup the 20 per cent charge through Social Security payments. However, experience on the ground suggests that the regulations are drawn so tightly that very few people are held to be in 'real' need. Can I pretend that this injustice is compatible with loving my neighbour or should I take advantages presented to me to raise the injustice publicly?

The very idea of making everyone, however poor, pay 20 per cent towards their Community Charge in the name of responsibility is a gross misunderstanding of what it is like to be trapped in poverty. I believe it is the calling of those of us in the Church who witness these things to publicise them as widely as possible. Especially as the evidence is that a large proportion of the people with the power to change things simply have no idea of what some of the people in this country suffer from our system.

We had an illustration of this in our part of the country around the time of the 1987 General Election. A local candidate engaged in a well-publicised exercise seeking to prove that Social Security benefits available were more than adequate to live on so long as a careful budget was followed and money was not wasted (a blow at the 'ciggies and beer scroungers' the tabloids love to hate). For a night or two our television screens carried images of the young hopeful shopping with his family in some well-stocked supermarket, and solemnly returning avocados to their display with the admonition that they were on a budget now and must watch what they ate. He was in debt by the end of one week without, it seems, having to bear the expense of major items such as clothing or quarterly bills. There was certainly no account taken of the stress of long-term lack of resources where everything wears out and nothing but the most essential items can be replaced – and then only with the cheapest and flimsiest of goods – with the result that people are drawn into an ever-deepening spiral of depression and debt. Most of us never bother to imagine what it means, for instance, to have an old burner, the one source of cooking food for a family, rendered useless in some accident and then be lent the money for a replacement rather than have access to an emergency grant. Repayments of a few pounds a month may seem perfectly manageable to those of us in waged employment, but if you are struggling to keep a family of three or four on the limited benefit available, such repayments may well finally sink you. They will certainly add stress and worry to the individuals concerned in ways that most people would consider vastly disproportionate to the savings made by the bureaucracy. The question arises: which is more important? The crushing of the individual person who might have been a resource to society, or the saving of money which may well prove a fool's saving when the result is to help pin that person in the trap of ever-deepening debt and depression?

The moral of the tale is that it is all too easy for those of us who are comfortably off – for all our regular little worries about how we are to pay for this 'necessary' item or that unexpected bill – to imagine that if we were one of the anonymous and burdensome poor, we should manage our affairs better. Until you have spent quite some considerable time either living with poverty or listening to the individual stories of fellow human beings, with their catalogue of minor irritations and small disasters writ large, accompanied by the crushing weight of depression which is the everyday experience of those lacking money in our society, you cannot begin to get a sense of this reality.

This is why the 1985 *Faith in the City* report was so important to us in the Church of England. It reminded us that the messages that dominate the lives of many, many people living in our deprived inner-city areas are that if you are poor, you do not count, you are a problem, society does not want you, school cannot prepare you for a job, and any neighbourliness is, in most cases, hard-won if available at all.

The reception of this report from the Archbishop's Commission on Urban Priority Areas, revealed just how far the Church was to find itself and its traditional Gospel in opposition to the 'spirit of the age'. The mid-80s were particularly a time of aggressive 'go-ahead' optimism, and the press, on behalf of Joe Public, did not take kindly to reminders of the wilderness that still lies in the heart of our cities. The accusations of Marxism that seeped in from some quarters recalled forcibly the remark of Dom Helder Camarra, a priest who worked in the midst of immense poverty in north-east Brazil. He once commented: 'When I give bread to the poor I am praised for my charity; if I ask – why do the poor have no bread? they call me a communist.' Personally, I found the report to be part of the same sober laying-out of experience and ignored facts as I aim to be part of.

At Easter 1988 I got into trouble again with the media for contributing to a news item about the new Social Security reforms that came in that year. I was once again told off in no uncertain terms for sullying people's enjoyment of a holy religious festival by leaping feet first into a contentious political debate.

The Social Security Reform Act of 1988 came into effect the week following Easter Sunday. It so happened that that year Easter Day followed soon after the announcement of the Spring Budget which seemed to have money to give away in tax cuts. The declared intention of the Government in bringing in the 1988 Social Security reforms was to streamline the range of benefits available and implement 'targeting'. The Budget they followed had just delivered tax cuts particularly targeted at the higher end of the wage-earning scale. I was being presented at the time with evidence from my own diocese, and from other people I knew and trusted who were working in deprived areas up and down the country, that the Social Security changes were going to make many poor people much poorer. While these changes were being brought in on the ideological pretext of enabling people to be free, there were unquestionable signs that a certain section of our population was having its freedom, opportunities and hopes further constricted.

I found the combination of Budget and Social Security changes focused for me an increasing disquiet. Declared Government policy appeared to place too great emphasis on those individuals who were free to make money so that they could make more money. There seemed a clear trend towards squeezing the poor in order to let the rich get richer. Given my faith and my belief I could not but see this as pretty immoral. There comes a point where people who celebrate Easter and take it seriously must ask themselves about love, justice, service and peace and how these things can be reconciled with what is actually being done in the society they live in – all the more when it is being done in their name as a citizen of a democracy. I faced that point and decided to accept the invitation of the Radio 4 news programme, *The World This Weekend*, to be interviewed in a piece on the way Government policy was going to mark the implementation of the new Social Security Reform Act – an item that was broadcast that Easter Sunday.

Part of the annoyance this interview caused, seems to have arisen from my use of a good old-fashioned theological term, that is: 'wicked'. True to form I went down in press files as having called the Prime Minister and her Cabinet wicked. This I did not do. I said the policies being promoted in the specific instance under discussion were 'verging on the wicked'. Calling in question the effect of policies, which appear to be taking from the poor in a time of so-called national prosperity, is not the same as attacking individual persons – even if they are politicians. I would not dream of calling in question anyone's motivation or their Christianity. I know that if I were not a Christian despite what I did wrong, there would be no hope. However, if national policies are making the better off, better off, and at the same time making the worse off, worse off – and these policies continue to be pursued apparently for theoretical reasons – then they are verging on the wicked and this must be faced.

I was reinforced in this belief by the extraordinary flood of mail I received in the days following the broadcast. In that week some 1100 letters arrived. Nine out of ten of them thanked me for speaking out. Many, many of them bore courageous and terrible personal testimony to the fears and debilitating hardships a broad section of people were facing because of the path our society was following. Young parents desperate for work yet unable to find it, feeling worthless and reviled for that failure in a society which glorified 'enterprise' and equated the possession of money with worth. Pensioners who spoke of sleepless nights worrying about the then forthcoming Poll Tax and turning off their fires, although they needed the warmth, because lack of money forced them to choose between heating and food. It was perhaps the most humbling and depressing postbag I have yet received. Humbling because of my inadequacy to respond. I had, after all, only spoken on a radio programme – there is little credit in that. Depressing because one of the phrases which kept being repeated in these letters was 'Thank God somebody in a position of influence has finally spoken up.' I found it, and still in retrospect find it, almost unbelievable that mine was being portrayed as a solitary voice. These things were pretty evident and widely supported by experts, professionals and detailed academic reports. Yet the story died, and the voice of all those hundreds of correspondents who bothered to write to me was barely registered in the babble of gossip, innuendo, political speculation and, at times, sheer propaganda, which seemed to form a greater part of so much of our news media.

The Social Security Reform Act of 1988, including the so-called 'targeting' and the replacement of the emergency grants by loans, has been in place for over two years now. The Poll Tax has also been implemented. And what about the consequences? According to the prophets of the Old Testament an unjust society brings chaos and instability down on itself. We are in an increasingly divided society and if a significant section of people are increasingly neglected (and there seems to be growing general acceptance that we are creating an underclass of people who are left out, forced out and who have dropped out) then it is not difficult to imagine that we may well be creating a festering pool of social anger. If you spend enough time reading reports from concerned groups and talking to people who work in the deprived areas, you can begin to wonder why more explosions have not taken place. We have, of course, seen Poll Tax riots and prison protests on our screens. Most of us dismiss them as isolated and extraordinary incidents. Perhaps we notice reports of rising crime figures and heave a sigh for the wicked times we live in. Maybe we even note signs of protest from a police force which feels itself increasingly inadequate to contain the anti-social elements of our population – but we probably tuck our worries away in the pigeonhole marked 'the law and order debate'. However, I think that – quite apart from my own faith and perception of what it is to be human – the Old Testament prophets had something. I believe it is mere common sense and prudence to acknowledge that a civilised and stable society in changing times requires a good deal more thought and emphasis on caring than we are giving it at the moment.

So the pressure of the facts combines with the basic community dynamic of God and the Gospel to make it clear that the Church cannot keep out of politics if it is to pursue the two great commandments of love of God and love of the neighbour.

The Church will find itself more and more involved in what might be called 'direct' politics the more politics become polarised and the more there seems to be a tendency for a particular political and social approach to go unchecked and unbalanced. At the moment it looks as if over-stress on the communal and collective has precipitated our society into over-stress on the individual and the private. The Church has an independent concern, arising from the worship of God and commitment to the Kingdom, about human living and human flourishing. So when either society or politics shows signs of polarisation (such as intensive militancy about particular political solutions or increasing statistical evidence of two nations) then the Church's political involvement will be heightened.

There are resources available to develop ordinary decent neighbourliness and helpfulness. The resources are the love and care of which all human beings are capable, reinforced by the love and care of God. When the direction of society seems to be crushing these resources rather than releasing them, then Christian leaders and individuals will keep being pushed into conflict with those in power, for they worship a God who is to be found through the love of the neighbour and celebrated in the worth of all persons.

I am a Christian and I am increasingly convinced that the Christian story and faith about God, men and women and the world, is a source of vital and necessary insights about what it is to be human. This is not to say that believers in God can make a monopolistic claim to total and exclusive truth about the world and being human. Faith in the God who is as He is in Jesus requires us to ask ourselves: What really matters? Where do we locate whatever faith we have and whatever value and worth we perceive? As St Augustine might have said – where do you find and focus your love – that is, the central commitment and attraction of your being? Because I feel by faith in God that God is the open mystery whom we, as beings created in His image, reflect, I am clear that such people cannot be shut up in any definition or label, and the worth of people must never be discarded in favour of any theory. What is of fundamental importance is God and human beings – men and women, all persons, including ourselves – not theories, visions, or doctrines of being human, except insofar as they are related and relatable to the promotion of being human. This is a concern that arises from the biblical injunctions against idolatry and this is what I turn to next.

8

False Gods and False Accounting

◆

I sometimes feel something of the confusion of the boy in the story who called out that the king had no clothes. I cannot be the only one to have watched with some perplexity as our vocabulary has undergone a radical change along with our politics in the last few years. Having always been interested in language, and how the use of words both shapes and reflects our assumptions, I must confess that it worries me when people are defined as consumers and something called the Market lurks in the background of every 'serious' political discussion, like some omnipresent deity. The Market, though rarely discussed in detail, is assumed to be real. So much so, that even so-called 'opposition' groups have slipped into the jargon almost unnoticed. Perfectly serious questions about the fact that the Market is, in reality, a theoretical abstraction to do with an interacting set of markets and other circumstances, seem to be ignored. As a result, political debates tend to suffer from confusion and a feeling of talking at cross-purposes. There has been a sort of emasculation of democratic debate whereby everyone worries details to death to little purpose because somehow the questioning of the assumptions that frame the debates has been rendered taboo. There has been such a triumph of one brand of political thinking that it has almost achieved the ultimate transformation of presenting itself not as a political philosophy, but as a summary of 'common sense', therefore reality.

We have reached a stage where all those who refuse to adopt the common assumptions are said to be unrealistic, woolly or simply blatantly wrong. It is said that true reality can be grasped in 'the bottom line'; what cannot be calculated and specified in public life is not real and therefore not worth discussing. We have had a radical revolution whereby the Augean stables of liberal confusion and socialist anarchy have been swept out. Old, slothful, misguided Britain has been shaken up, straightened out, tidied up and set on the plain, common sense path to prosperity. Revolution is not quite the right word – revelation might be more appropriate. The leap of faith has been made from the notion that a theory is a way of getting to grips with the world in a partial and practical way, to the belief that one particular economic theory describes in a sufficiently complete manner how the world actually goes on. The implication is that we have cracked the code of the proper organisation of human flourishing – or at least, we have produced a pretty good sketch of how the world works. We are told – this is reality, there is no alternative. Having been convinced by my own religious revelation, I have my doubts. For a Christian, to say there is no alternative is a form of practical atheism because it denies the hope that is always there if you really believe in God.

Here may I declare my political colours. I feel impelled by my faith to raise questions about the current dominant political philosophy. That dominant political philosophy is the Market philosophy of the present Government. I therefore stand opposed to many of the principles on which the Right Wing of politics in our country rest. However, exactly where I stand in the present political spectrum is difficult to say. There is nowhere much to stand – that is part of the problem. As somebody said in a review of one of my books, had I lived in a Socialist State I would probably have been busy criticising the idolatry of the State instead of the idolatry of the Market. My problem with politics is that I do not believe politics can bring in the Kingdom of God. If I must be defined in political terms, I am in favour of pragmatic, consensus politics. I am not, as I have been told by some people, a Marxist. Marx raised some pertinent criticisms that need to be taken seriously. However, one of the things that I find most irritating about some of the more Right Wing elements of our political circles these days, is that they almost make it look as if Marx was right by producing and working on a mirror-image of his economic determinism. Nevertheless, I remain convinced he was wrong in his conclusions.

Given the assault on Christian principles represented by the core of Market philosophy, it does seem a little naïve for some politicians to express surprise that the Church should be forced into open opposition. At the moment we live in a climate of opinion which maintains that messages and morality about people as persons of worth – however powerful and moving – cannot operate beyond the personal, face to face level. Market philosophy claims that the market system is the only effective information system we have for aggregating out results, across all the complexity of individual choices, local circumstances and interacting transactions across the world, in such a way as to achieve the best survival, welfare and prosperity possible for mankind.

This is a claim about the realities of the world and the possibilities of human beings. Therefore it must be a philosophy which is of interest and concern to a convinced Christian, particularly when its assumptions come to dominate the life of the society of which we are part. The Christian churches exist because there is a fundamental conviction both that God is the ultimate reality and that God has revealed Himself to people in the realities of their particular lives and circumstances. Consequently, any view of the world that claims there is a 'spontaneous human order' (in the words of the Market philosopher Hayek) which determines how we should see things and respond to things is bound to be of quite crucial interest to all Christians.

In pure Market philosophy, for instance, justice is not a social concept. The contention is that we cannot come to a consensus as to what is 'just', therefore justice can only be an ordering concept administered by the minimal state to do with the preservation of property and the preservation of private, individual space, so that Market choices and what is termed 'individual freedom' may be preserved. This is to be done regardless of whatever imaginary and utopian dreams may lurk at the back of human minds – however powerful these longings may be – about humanity as some sort of family, or society as a real organisation in which citizenship could operate towards mutually organised caring.

To put this argument into Christian language, the concept of Market philosophy involves the assumption that the Kingdom of God is not applicable to running human affairs in an extended order – that is at institutional, organisational and global levels. This is not new. In the eighteenth century the philosopher Hume made the same point. He argued that the great commandments were all very well at the individual level but if they were allowed to interfere with the State, economic and other affairs they were as mischievous as any set of villains. Robert Owen, the nineteenth-century reformer, picked up the argument in a gentler form, remarking that Jesus was probably the most important and powerful person who ever lived but that what he had brought into the world could not cope with nineteenth-century industry and its effects. Hayek, the grand old man of the twentieth-century Market philosophers, agrees with Hume and quotes – with some approval – a 'nineteenth-century enthusiast' who said that the most important book since the Bible – and which had practically replaced the Bible – was Adam Smith's *Wealth of Nations*. The feeling, therefore, is that reality has proved that personal, biblically based, morality – such as loving your neighbour – is actually detrimental to human flourishing if applied at more than the personal, face to face, level. In the words of Hayek, 'An order in which everyone treated his neighbour as himself would be one where comparatively few would be fruitful and multiply' (Hayek, *Socialism, the Fatal Conceit*). This is a philosophy that denies we can love our neighbours through the way we organise our society.

The radical reforms of our national institutions introduced by the present Government focus a central human question which is an issue in all our political disputes and deserves great attention, despite its complexity. (Now, I am aware of the neat and perceptive remark that 'most Englishmen would die rather than think, and many of them do.' Nevertheless, it is my contention that we must apply our reason – however painful that might be – if we are to take hold of our fate and steer towards some sort of hopeful future.) This central question is: does realism demand that there are two separate tiers of relationships – one at the level of institutions and global relations and the other of personal, face to face relations – or, can and should these two levels be inter-related and inseparable?

It is my belief that the present trend of political reforms conceal a challenge about what sort of undertaking being a citizen could or might be, and about what sort of messages we can share with one another as citizens.

Take the example of the National Health Service and the current reform proposals which are, at the time of writing, being initially put into effect after passing through Parliament. The NHS was set up as a kind of keystone of an attempt to build and maintain the post-war Welfare State. The Welfare State has progressed from having problems and limitations in practice to a bad press in general, but the current attempts to reorganise face us directly with a fundamental question of where we, as a community, place our priorities. The Beveridge Welfare Plan of the 1940s was a serious communal attempt to do something about certain 'demons' which constantly threaten substantial numbers of our fellow citizens. Demons of acute want, fear of the effects of ill health and the crippling effects of unemployment. The NHS could be said to be a sort of touchstone about the way we regard citizenship, its possibilities, its duties and its rights. It is also of very direct, personal and individual significance. Members of my generation, who can remember back before the institution of the Welfare State, are vividly aware of what the establishment of health care for all, when in need and without reference to cost at the time of need, meant. I was very conscious as a young man that one of the benefits I enjoyed in contrast to my father was that, having found the person I wanted to marry, I did not have the problem of deciding whether I was earning enough to risk the considerable doctor's bills involved in supporting a wife and family. In the old days sickness was not only a health problem but also an extremely threatening economic one.

Much has gone wrong over costs and the organisation of the Welfare State, but was the undertaking to set up sufficient means of protecting all citizens from the worst onslaughts of misfortune wrong in principle? Do we now reject that as citizens we should acknowledge together some responsibility for each other? And can we really dismiss these considerations merely by saying that we cannot afford them?

Perhaps you feel that these questions are overly dramatic. We are all committed to the NHS but it is very wasteful. Resources are limited – after all, we as tax payers foot the bill, and we are not prepared to keep on paying out. The institution must be made more efficient. This is what the reforms are about.

Along with most of the medical profession and many other people, I agree that the institution needs reforming. The present Government has raised important questions about efficiency, costs, and organisation. However, the proposals are not merely about making the institution more efficient. They are radical reforms shaped by a philosophy which is alien to the principles on which the NHS was founded. The Welfare State arose from some sort of generally understood consensus about shared social purposes. The present Government feels that the stress should be on individual responsibility and private choice. The claim is that this stress does not involve ditching the other, communal concern. I would argue that on present evidence, it does.

The Government reforms are focused around the gathering of technical information about the running of the NHS and establishing market procedures into this running. The common sense of this seems obvious. We have limited resources. We should therefore discover, and keep track of, the cost of everything – how else can we find where money is being wasted and make sure we are using our resources to the maximum effect? But it is not that simple. Some things are hard to cost and some things our present accounting procedures simply do not take account of. For instance, you can now come across charts which demonstrate 'product' flows through a particular hospital department. That may seem fairly straightforward until you consider that the 'products' referred to are, perhaps, sick women or children. This will not do. Sick human beings are not consumers; their medical care and treatment is not a product. There are, in human relations and social services, unquantifiable things which cannot have price tags fixed to them, and yet are vital in preserving the space necessary to being human and treating each other as human beings should be treated. That is, as individual persons of worth, not consuming machines.

I once came across a simply splendid spoof diagram, in one of the magazines that drug companies produce, which demonstrated quite clearly that the NHS would run perfectly well if you could just remove the patients. I sometimes feel that this is the kind of unspoken ethos behind many of the reforms. The information systems they seek to establish operate solely on technical messages to the extent where human messages can only distort them. The reform proposals are directed towards producing sophisticated systems of costing and billing, the rapid production of detailed audits and detailed business plans – all aimed to allow managers and organisers to make informed choices. This again sounds like excellent common sense and good housekeeping, but the side-effects cannot be ignored. You can cost to the last penny the amount of drugs you use, the cost of theatre time and bed space, but you cannot pin down the cost of that extra bit of flexibility that gives doctors and nurses the space to respond when a patient needs reassurance or simply to have someone be with them a while. Flexibility which makes all the difference to medical care and the recovery of patients. Then there is the broader question, as a report from the Church of England's Board of Social Responsibility on the White Paper put it – 'What will happen to the trust between a doctor and a patient if the decision to treat is inextricably bound up with the decision to spend?'

The narrow cash basis of the accounting procedures presently being applied is inadequate to the ethos of the institution they are supposed to reform. These procedures are threatening to dominate the Health Service as if it were a market for health care consumption rather than a social institution for caring for all in health need, as and when they suffer.

This may not be the intention but it seems to be what is actually happening. I repeat, many of the questions being raised are very sensible. Certainly the NHS and other organisations should benefit from advances in technology. Yet I fail to see why, if these sophisticated systems can deliver such information, it cannot be used to run the NHS more efficiently on its present lines and within an overall concern for people, rather than with this great ideological shift in the narrowly market direction.

Some people will no doubt ask – why get so worked up about a simple change of language? Because language changes, though subtle, have a pernicious effect. To classify human beings as either products or consumers is to degrade them. Effect of language is cumulative and it is easy to dismiss such concerns as mere pedantic fussing. However I am convinced that the infiltration of business language into politics is a symptom of an important change in perspective which has come to blunt the edges of crucial human questions. For the fashionable terms are not just arbitrary or cosmetic. They arise from a coherent philosophy which has risen to the level of a faith. A faith that the Market is the solution to all our economic problems, and that economic relations are the only quantifiable and real relations that bind human beings beyond the limited circles of family and face to face relationships.

What is is that the application of Free Market principles is supposed to offer? The answer seems to be – prosperity. Is it not the Market Economies, based on individual enterprise, that have delivered the prosperity and general superiority in freedom and the pursuit of happiness, of the Western civilisations? And has this system not finally been proved to be the best by current events in which we see the Eastern bloc, the bastion of Socialism, crumbling and its peoples rushing to convert to the 'truth' about prosperity and human flourishing?

Contrary to what people might think, I am certainly not against wealth creation, nor the application of Market principles in their place; however, I do ask whether we really are seeing the triumph of Capitalism or whether the West might not find itself going West, just as the East tumbles to join it. Should we not look at this prosperity we have produced – what kind it is and where it has brought us?

The spectacular development of the Metro Shopping and Leisure Centre near Gateshead represents something of the deep ambiguity of our present notion of prosperity. Go there on any day of the week and the arcades and leisure centre are filled with window gazers and shoppers. Anything that brings movement, imagination, a few jobs and a sense of something being done in the area must be welcomed as a morale booster. Yet no one seems to ask how permanent is the apparent transformation. How long can a centre which contains such a high percentage of service industries and shops continue to flourish unless there is a steady increase in income in the surrounding communities from which it draws its customers? This is a fundamental question, quite apart from more immediate considerations such as how the present success will withstand the transition when subsidies, such as those attached to the Enterprise Zone Scheme, run out and businesses have to pay the full Community Charge business rate.

There is ambiguity, too, within the operation itself. The centre has created new jobs, but these are not the same kind of jobs as the manufacturing employment that has disappeared at such a rate over the last decade or so. The new service industries and retail businesses that fill the malls employ a large percentage of part-time and casual labour at what are generally accepted to be pretty low wages. So the rise in the number of jobs created is not necessarily matched by any equivalent real achievement in the wealth and well-being of the wage-earners. There is uncertainty too about what effect, in the longer term, such out-of-town shopping centres have on the communities around them. There are signs that they drain business from local corner shops to the extent where many have to close. Small shops and post offices, once centres of local life, disappear to the disadvantage of the poor and relatively immobile members of society such as the elderly and mothers with young children. Such effects may well be contributing to killing off what might be termed the strictly local economy, which is an important part of sustaining community in areas such as ex-pit villages, and small towns, where economic shifts are making it increasingly difficult for communities to survive. There are signs that our way of prospering is contributing to sealing off a certain minority of people in 'excluded' zones.

Whatever the qualifications, the North East has certainly benefited from the economic boom that has crossed our country over the last decade. New shops display stylish clothes and consumables, smart trading estates have sprung up sporting twenty-first-century structures decked out in primary colours, and urban regeneration has begun to lift the face of many of our inner cities. Yet what about the spread of this new wealth? After some ten years of the application of the Market revolution, the 'trickle-down' theory does not seem to be having marked success in my part of the world. Not only do perhaps up to thirty per cent of the population seem to remain poor and excluded but also the gap between rich and poor is getting wider. If you take a trip down the River Wear that runs through my diocese you can see vivid illustration of this. On the south side is Hendon, a struggling and poor community. In the churches we are involved in a number of efforts trying to assist groups of people there in tapping their own resources of self-help and skill. On the other side of the river, Government-funded development agencies are co-ordinating the private sector development of a marina with high-quality housing, leisure facilities and business hotels. I am clear that the people working for these development corporations are well-intentioned and doing all they can to bring prosperity to the area, but still I have to raise questions about the people who are left in Hendon on the other side of the river – their poverty untouched and themselves excluded from the forced prosperity blooming tantalisingly on the opposite bank. It is not for lack of trying, but leisure, it seems, is just not that productive and recycled wealth just does not trickle down far enough. Perhaps the economic theory is inadequate to the task of making inroads into endemic poverty.

Then there is the question of whether this wealth we have created can be sustained. Short-term booms are not necessarily transformations. The mechanism of the Market depends on competition. In practice competition in economic matters means rapid obsolescence. Evidence of this can be seen on the trading estates around my diocese in the high turn-over of businesses. This is a world-wide experience – 'booms' in particular industries move with increasing rapidity from West to East where wages are much lower and workers more exploited.

Competition, in crude terms, is fuelled by the battle of dog eat dog. Those who fail in the competition game are pushed out of it or get taken over. The evidence is that, due to their wealth and cash resources, this system favours the creation of ever bigger multi-national corporations. It is a natural consequence of this process that, in the North East as elsewhere, much of the new-found prosperity is dependent on firms based outside the region – often companies with headquarters half a world away. The pressures of competition and financial viability mean that multi-national companies do not have the flourishing of local economies very high on their list of priorities. When economic advantage dictates that they close down a factory and move else-where – they do so, despite the fact that their withdrawal throws the economy of the community they leave behind into chaos.

Then there is the growth factor. Another reality of the free market system is that there would be no growth without credit. Yet do we ever ask who bears the cost of this credit system? The other side of the growth coin is the real human misery witnessed to in this country by the steadily increasing numbers of desperate persons who, at present, are overloading our Citizens Advice Bureaux and other advisory charities. I see evidence of this everywhere in estates where my fellow priests and others serve. On the global scale the misery is even greater. As I know, for instance, from a bishop friend of mine in Uganda. Once upon a time Uganda could support itself. Now it has to grow cash crops in order to pay its debts, and people starve. You might argue – 'But all these people, both as individuals and as countries, borrowed this money, they should be more responsible.' But when a system is fostering such a lot of human misery can you really pretend that we in the West have no responsibility for the system we have created, which is making many of 'us' rich, while 'they' starve?

We are told that the Market's way of wealth creation is the only system capable of creating the wealth to lift the Third World and the poor in general out of their poverty. But is it? Is free market economics up to the challenge of endemic poverty? The evidence at present seems to be that the market mechanism of credit and debt reinforces the poor in the poverty trap.

Then what about the environmental challenges we face today? How is our so-called enterprise relating to the needs of the environment and the future? Is our present system up to the pressure of the facts now before us?

Anyone travelling along the coast of my diocese will be forcibly reminded of how our ways of production are damaging our earth. The chemical works at Billingham turn the sky yellow with the fumes seeping from their towers. On a cloudy day it becomes quite suffocating. Yet Billingham needs the jobs the chemical factories provide. To close them down would destroy the local economy. This is the argument advanced for ignoring the pollution. We must live with it; the priorities of profit and jobs are more important in the short term.

In the short term. Here we come to another major problem of the free market system. The Market is not concerned with the long-term future. The Market is focused on buying and dealing and profit-taking. In the entrepreneurial society, choices are made here and now with a view to survival in the market place here and now. Enterprises have to be focused on making sure that their 'bottom line' balances are sufficient to immediate survival and profit. The fact that the emissions involved in the processes of production may be poisoning the air we breathe, is not part of the entrepreneurial world. There is no immediate and direct consequence of such ways of going on; people are not yet choking to death in the streets. Consumers keep buying the products and the producers keep making a profit. The manufacturers are not the ones to bear the costs of cleaning up. Why should they? Altruism of that kind would merely drive them into bankruptcy and someone else would take their place (another illustration of the argument against neighbourliness at a business level). And yet, the pollution keeps mounting while we make little more than cosmetic adjustments to our production processes.

Surely someone should regulate? According to the law of the free market, the role of the State should be minimal and is to do as much deregulation as possible while maintaining some sort of eye on standards. Regulation will come naturally because producers and consumers alike will discover it to be in their interests. This is the theory, but where is the evidence? At recent conferences the Western Governments agreed a formula on the phasing out of ozone-depleting chemicals which, in effect, means that emissions will be held at present levels until well into the next century. Scientists have concrete evidence that this policy is sheer folly. We are told that the Market and consumers will perceive their common self-interest and all will be well in the end. This is a matter of faith. Yet there is no evidence to support this faith.

Too many of the present people in power seem dogmatically convinced that they have the ideological key to what is going on and what ought to be done. Firm in this conviction, they are not prepared to listen to arguments which can reasonably claim to show that their policies and actions can be questioned, or that these policies have demonstrable effects other than those which their proponents claim or want to recognise. Statistics on poverty, for instance, can be dismissed as either incorrect or irrelevant. Evidence about the increasing accumulation of people in work at a low level of wages may be explained away. However, in the consequences of our environmental depredations we are presented with challenges so urgent they cannot be brushed aside.

The present evidence is clear – we are coming up against the limits to growth. We are in danger of polluting ourselves into extinction by the waste we produce. Yet we remain wedded to a system based on competitive growth. Competition creates waste. Not only the wasted enterprise of the losers in the competitive game, but all the waste created by the throwaway culture necessary to fuel the growth in consumption by which the system measures its success.

Perhaps we cannot see into the future to see whether the alarming projections of scientists will be proved right about the ozone layer and global warming, but we have examples of the common sense need to question this growth principle before us on our roads. Anyone trying to get round London in a taxi these days has plenty of time to reflect on the destructive effects of affluence as we now understand it, and freedom as it is now promoted. There is a famous passage of the ancient historian Tacitus in his work on the Britons which says that the Romans 'solitudinem faciunt et pacem appellant', which means 'they make a desert and they call it peace'. Today's paraphrase might be: 'they make a traffic jam and they call it prosperity'.

Common sense indicates that there are limits to the organisational powers of the free market for the benefit of mankind. If the pollution question is not threatening enough to make us rethink our assumptions, there is the depletion argument. From the 1960s, when the first images of the earth were broadcast from the Apollo satellite, we have known in crystal clear terms that we inhabit one limited earth, with limited resources. Publicity is at last beginning to get across the message that our exploitations and depredations are changing our weather systems and affecting the air we need to breathe, but, is action being taken fast enough? It is plain and obvious that the earth cannot sustain being treated as if it were nothing but a hunk of consumables. Are Market Economics flexible enough to adapt to challenges such these?

It is under these conditions that we are supposed to be celebrating the fact that the people of Eastern Europe have seen the light of free enterprise, and we are urging them to join our wasteful ways. Consider a moment. Suppose that the recent developments in Eastern Europe touch off a rapid growth boom (as we at present understand growth, in terms of rising standards of living based on greater consumption). Suppose, further, that the overflow effect of this was to start the Third World off on a similar path of accelerated growth and consumption. Could the earth sustain the results? The answer, simply and soberly, in view of the facts, must be 'no'.

We are going to have to face the real costs of our way of life. The evidence is before us and if we value the quality of life we are going to have to rethink. As the writer René du Bois used to point out in the early days of ecological writing, the real problem with the human race is not that it finds it difficult to survive but that, very regrettably, it is capable of surviving under the most intolerable conditions. Our assumptions may lead us to choke ourselves with pollution, overwhelm ourselves with the waste from our reckless consumption and allow our passion for cars to fossilise our cities and motorways, but we still cannot quite wipe life out. We may well, however, stop life being worth living.

It could be that all these problems are costs we are willing to bear, for according to the theory, free market philosophy is supposed to deliver political as well as economic advantages. It is claimed that it promotes, and indeed rests upon, individual choice and freedom. In March 1990, *The Times* published an interesting article in which a Government Minister set out, in fighting spirit, the aims and perceived achievements of the Government in its application of Market principles. He stated: 'For the past decade this Conservative Government has pressed forward with measures designed to increase individual freedom, responsibility and choice. Choice is how people spend the money they earn . . . The Conservative Government has stood back and encouraged people to live in the real world of individual choices where actions have consequences and costs, and individuals can see the link between the two.' The Government reforms, he was clear, were giving 'individuals more control over their own lives'.

Is this definition of real choice as depending on the possession of money adequate? How reliable a premise for 'freedom' is the possession of money? According to certain people we have achieved a state in our country where most of us have money. Even if this contention were to be accepted – even if we were all rich – would the criterion of money be a moral or even barely stable basis for freedom? And what sort of ideal and definition of freedom does this statement imply?

Who has freedom is one of the principal points at issue in the current debates about economic realities and political programmes. If choice is dependent on choosing how you spend the money you earn, what happens to those without money? Do the poor have their freedom constrained or removed by their poverty? Furthermore, if everything is ultimately determined by the Market, what happens to choice?

The whole matter of how people make choices and how you enable them to make choices is highly complex. We are into the realm of messages and what we think the world is about, how the world runs and how it can be helped to run. Choice, if it is to be real and valuable, needs to be informed – both about what is on offer and what might or could be on offer if people were organised to deliver it. But this is not what is actually being established.

It looks very much as if the most vulnerable are regularly losing by the application of free market philosophy. The notion, for instance, of shopping around for the best treatment on offer in a reformed NHS assumes considerable resources of energy and mobility. There are many prospective patients among the elderly and the poor who cannot easily travel. Even if the reforms allow choice over a wider geographical area, such people may well not be able to take advantage of that choice. If they do, they will not be visitable by their friends and relations because of the costs and difficulties of travel. The results will be fragmentation of community, threat to community care and diminishing concern for people who most need it. The bewildered, the inarticulate, the slow on the uptake, while they may be confused by the present system, are likely to be more confused by far, when it is demanded that they exercise such choice in an impersonal and remote system.

Despite the theory which claims to explain why selfishness in trade, commerce and market activity works to the best possible benefit of all, I find it difficult to ignore worries about freedom and power as they are actually experienced on the ground. It is the claim of the present dominant political philosophy that power is being dispersed so that the individual is left as free as possible to pursue his or her own choice within his or her means. Power, it is claimed, is being dispersed 'from the hub of the wheel to the rim'. However what seems to be being brought about is not just a dispersal of power, but a fragmentation of power. The only power that is not being fragmented is that of central government and big business. Under such conditions freedom becomes an increasingly dubious concept.

A government which claims to be in power in the interests of reducing the power and influence of government and the state is, apparently systematically, attacking, restricting and attempting to weaken all alternative centres of power and influence, other than the central government bureaucracy and a certain number of faceless, monopolistic, international corporations, far removed from face-to-face responsibility for the effect of their decisions on ordinary people.

Take, for instance, the demolishing of the power of the Unions. The Trade Unions have, in some ways, asked for it by their unresponsive tyranny over membership and a Luddite-style resistance to innovation and adaptation. But it is surely impractical nonsense to pretend that waged workers do not need a countervailing power to protect them against the impersonal and arbitrary decisions of remote owners or from local managers who have the same temptation as trade union leaders to exploit power. Selfish, stupid or undesirable exercises of power are not confined to the 'lower orders'.

Local Authorities have, for the last hundred years or so, developed into a counterweight to excessive centralisation of power in national government hands. What is happening to their role? Their influence is being reduced by the imposition of restrictions on the ways they raise money and even the way they spend the money they raise. Responsibility for, and control of, housing, education and other matters is being eroded by centrally imposed policies which promote the dispersal of properties and services to private control.

We pride ourselves on our democratic traditions. The exercise of democratic choice depends on access to information. Therefore the condition of our public news and broadcasting services are of crucial importance. Here too there are grounds, on the power and freedom front, to be concerned both about newspapers and about radio and television. Particularly on the evidence of press and communication empires amassing in the monopolistic direction, because of the scale of the finances which are now required to launch and maintain either a national newspaper, or a regional or national television station. There are signs, too, that the dominant pressure of financial considerations in a 'free market' promotes the emphasis on entertainment to the detriment of the socially important services of accurate and unbiased news reporting and programming reflecting issues of public debate.

Then there is the assault on professional bodies and independent institutions. The countervailing power of these arose from the way they were organised as power and pressure groups, their prestige and their being funded to a certain extent by public taxation. This funding left them independence and control over the ways they spent their budgets. Now all such institutions – universities, the NHS, the public broadcasting service – are targets for attack on grounds of efficiency, cost-effectiveness and accusations that they are unable to meet the current needs of society and business. Both funding and control are to be passed increasingly to dispersed and privatised centres or bodies. Whatever the weight of the real questions about economic efficiency and flexibility within these institutions, the clear upshot of these attacks is to diminish what independence and influence they once had. With guaranteed financial resources being steadily reduced and the pressures of raising money through voluntary measures, market measures or patronage, more and more power is given to those with money. Those who believe they stand outside these institutions and the professions that serve them may well think – 'And about time too'. However, it is worth taking a look at what is replacing these countervailing powers. It is not individual freedom.

The ordinary citizen, in his or her locality, is becoming more and more a mere individual unit with no opportunity to bring any countervailing power to bear on what is ordered from Whitehall or being decided by controllers of industrial corporate money and resources. The power of central government and the power of the wealthy commercial conglomerations is rising, and everyone else is being stripped of resource or countervailing centres of influence which might be brought to bear on the current game called 'Free Enterprise' – an enterprise set free by government action which steadily squeezes any other enterprise out of existence either by regulation or monetary deprivation. Free enterprise is then left to go on what is alleged to be its 'own' way, but is in fact a way determined by an increasingly interlocked group of limited corporations whose members, individually or corporately, control the immense sums of money which are now required to have any noticeable effect in this 'Free Enterprise'.

The Market philosophers visualise 'the Market' as an 'extended order', an evolved communications system of trade, production, exchange and consumption, within which all the component and interacting parts are apparently assumed to be of roughly equal weight. The application of the theory to reality shows this is not so. The problem and threat of size, dominance and power in commercial companies is indicated by the steadily shrinking list of leading companies through the growth and merging of multi-national companies. In the shadow of such giants, the multiplication of small businesses or of small share-holders would seem to be purely cosmetic with relation to issues of power and freedom. The reality is that 'free market' forces produce massive groupings, monopolies, and multi-national conglomerates, which distort the power and freedom flow all one way, and distort the messages of the system over-whelmingly to reflect their own short-term interests. The 'free market', therefore, becomes increasingly a cipher or even a deceit.

For all the rhetoric about freedom of choice for the individual, what appears to be happening is that, on the pretext of being free to consume, we are being stripped of all our other free-doms. Past definitions of democracy, freedom, choice – matters crucial to being human in a society – are being redefined in the blinking of an eye. The debate about what it is to be human has been closed with the banal and unimaginative formula that man is defined by his ability to consume. After some 500 years of Western civilisation, man has been diverted from the old goals of liberty, fraternity, equality and democracy and, in exchange for a few consumer goods, is allowing himself to be stripped of all but the freedom to consume – if, that is, he is first fortunate enough to have the ability to earn the money necessary for par-ticipation in our consumer society.

Are the benefits we gain from this exchange worth the costs that stare us in the face if we but look up from our immediate comforts and concerns? Costs such as social division, the erosion of democracy, irreparable ecological devastation, and human beings starving in the Third World to pay interest on debts which can never be paid off while the Western banks build ever larger monuments to commerce and financial success.

There is a need to challenge that trend in society which reflects selfish consumerism. Consumerism is the modern, and seemingly highly organised version, of the basic and perennial sin of Pleonexia (Greek) or Concupiscentia (Latin). Pleonexia means the condition and dynamic of wanting more and more. We need to come to terms with the fact that, as religious people through the ages have always said, the bare-faced pursuit of selfish, immediate, individual satisfaction is morally, personally and socially destructive.

We are what we consume in a rather terrible way. We have consumed the idea that status can be valued in monetary terms: this notion has turned on us and reflected back the creeping assumption that people are valued for what they are worth in monetary terms. To be concerned about this is not a matter of being 'against consumption'. I too enjoy having enough money to take a holiday, to be able to buy a bottle of wine or purchase some of the fascinating books that are published these days – all those things that add pleasure to life and lift it out of being a grind. Having sufficient money gives a certain spaciousness to existence, it enables you to get around and enjoy life to the full. What is destructive is when consumption becomes an idol to the extent where the meaning of life is reduced to consumption.

In the Old Testament, the Prophet Isaiah described how following false gods led Judah to a parlous state.

> How the faithful city has played the whore.
> Once the home of justice where righteousness dwelt
> Now murderers dwell.
> Your silver has turned to base metal
> And your liquor is diluted with water
> Your very rulers are rebels
> Confederate with thieves
> Every man of them loves a bribe and itches for a gift

They do not give the orphan his rights
And the widow's cause never comes before them

(From Isaiah, 1: 21–23)

The prophets generally had a pretty sharp way of putting things. It is, of course, ridiculous to draw parallels with our modern society – or is it?

Where has our way of going on brought us? We have a society where an increasingly impoverished underclass of fellow human beings is taken for granted as inevitable. We are told that neighbourliness must 'be affordable' yet we redefine 'affordable' in ever more selfish terms. It seems to be more and more taken for granted that threats to the interests of 'me and my group' justify almost any response of anger, frustration, indifference to the interests of other wider groups and total short-sightedness about longer term effects. If we are doing well then any suggestion that we should be regulated, taxed or invited to contribute more to some common endeavour is treated as an assault on our freedom, ideological nonsense, or sentimental do-goodery – whatever the effects of our particular 'doing well' may be on the welfare of others. Money is for those who can make it and those who cannot make it must not be allowed to get in the way of its being made. Morality and caring are separated from money-making and considered solely as matters for individual choice and responsibility.

But where has such an approach brought us? As a society we are showing signs of falling apart into quarrelling and quarrelsome groups. Compassion runs out increasingly quickly. We pride ourselves on the amount we give to charity yet our streets are filling with homeless. Our society reflects our gods of money and materialism – social division, an increasing chasm between the mobile rich and the ghettoised poor, rising crime figures and a pool of social anger and violence. Something is very wrong and very rotten. We are following false gods.

This is a matter of idolatry. Idolatry is manifested by many ways of commitment to the piling up of wealth and the irresponsible enjoyment of luxury – for self-indulgence and sensuousness are forms of idolatry. It is a matter of 'what you put your money on' or 'where do you place your love'. Do you place your trust in gods you can carry about so that you can fix them where it suits you, or do you put your faith in some transcendent Worth and God who is both with you and independent of you?

The question I am trying to raise is: what is it proper 'to have faith in'? Even if you do not believe in God, you cannot replace Him with an economic theory. It is, after all, well known that for economists the real world is always a special case. Economic theories are collections of perceptions and alleged matters of fact. Alleged matters of fact are not things to have faith in. They form empirical evidence which you may be reasonably convinced entitles you, or requires you, to rely on it and respond to it. To place your absolute faith in an economic theory is to court destruction.

One of the things I learn as I get older is that everybody thinks that their view of the world is the real one. But we are all wrong. None of us, actually, personally or professionally – however inspired we might be – picks up on the whole of reality. Reform is clearly necessary as society develops. The basic question is what informs the reform? Can we aim at being any particular sort of society with certain visions of responsibility and citizenship? The critical issue is that the current dominant answer to this is 'no'. There is, and can be, no consensus. It is my perception of the state we have come to in our society that this attitude is leading us into a very uncertain future. Unless we can rediscover community and the meaning of being in a society together, we cannot head in any very hopeful direction.

Worth is not equated with money – however banal that statement is, our society seems well on the way to forgetting it. Remember the tale of King Midas who thought that gold was the only thing he needed to make him happy. The gods cursed him with the gift whereby everything he touched turned to gold and he starved to death. An ancient truth that cannot lightly be ignored. It very much looks as if the price of our survival, given the present odds, involves a change in attitude, a change in habits and a change in priorities. This in theological language can be described as a call to repentance.

If you say there is no alternative you are saying there is no hope. Is this all that men and women have come to after so many thousand years of painful evolution? *Après moi le déluge?* The belief that we must carry on with our destructive ways because we have no choice has been common among human beings from the very earliest times. See the Prophet Jeremiah (18:12):

> But they answer, things are past hope
> We will do as we like
> And each of us will follow the promptings
> Of his own wicked and stubborn heart.

This could be said to be a remarkable characterisation of much in our society at the moment. However, according to the Christian understanding, things are never past hope. There is hope in being under judgement if in face of the reality exposed before you, you repent, rethink and change.

The Greeks long ago diagnosed a tendency in human and political affairs for those who gathered power to themselves to develop what the Ancients called 'hubris'. A form of overweening arrogance which led the powerful and successful person or group to become oblivious both to factual realities and to ordinary and social moral decencies. The way the Greeks told it, this led to 'ātē' – the downfall and destruction of the apparently powerful and successful through some set of tragic, stupid and accidental events and actions. At present, we have people in power who seem dogmatically convinced that they, and they alone, have the ideological key to what is going on and so to what ought to be done. They must not be allowed to get away with such hubris.

There is an urgent need for the issue of freedom to be kept in the forefront of public concern, investigation and discussion. Parties in power, whoever they are, simply must not be allowed to get away with the idea that their power includes the power to define reality or prescribe what freedom is. Such hubris is the

prelude both to developing tyranny and debilitating ineffi-
ciency, for it attempts to fit the intractabilities of human living
together into the trivialising routineness of a theory. Individual,
named, loving and suffering human beings become, for
example, either a mere expendable unit in the market process or
a mere expendable unit in the dialectical march towards the perfect community beyond the State. Communists in power have
done this, now Marketeers in power are attempting to do it.
Such attempts threaten to maim, if not destroy, both freedom
and true, risky and intractable humaneness.

It is a basic fact of life that unless we are prepared to confine
and decisively exclude those who disagree with us, societies
in times of profound change need some sort of trust. This
involves returning to some basic core of consensus. The problem of market-orientated policies is that they disregard trust and
consensus because they are directed by an ideology, and the
point about an ideology is that those who believe in it are convinced it contains the truth and must be followed at all costs.

The real world may not only be a special case for economists
but also a case which is particularly calling in question the 'fashionable' ideas of the Market. It seems to me quite possible that
capitalism and the Market, in the form we now know it, might
have had their two hundred or so years.

This is not to imply that the only alternative, if we are to
reject Market Capitalism, is to turn back to embrace Socialism. I
cannot accept that the only realistic world view is based on a
contest between Market Capitalism and Socialism – nor that
Capitalism can be said to have been proved right merely by the
collapse of Socialism. This is simply vulgar Marxism in reverse.
The Marxist doctrine speaks of the spurious freedom of the
bourgeoisie being at the expense of the real freedom of the
workers, hence the only way of universalising freedom is to
force the creation of a classless society after the withering away
of the State. The diagnosis of the new Right is a mirror image of
this. The spurious freedom is that of the Socialist collective of
the workers, which has been attempted at the expense of the
true freedom of the bourgeois individualists. It is this freedom
which is alone universalisable after the market has been

liberated to work its wonders and there emerges the freedom of a property-owning democracy while the State has been reduced to the absolute minimum.

The Hayekian description of the extended order is perhaps best described as an idealised version of a reasonably plausible and apparently descriptive account of trading and industrial affairs round about the time of Adam Smith. Smith's *Wealth of Nations*, which Hayek regards as so influential, was a reasonable and persuasive account of the system as seen from the perspective of those who fitted into and benefited from it in the eighteenth century. It was probably always an illusion that this ideal and extended order ever existed or worked as it is held to work. However useful the thought experiment of constructing and describing this extended order, so that the modelling involved can be used for analyses and practical suggestions in particular areas, it remains the case that the theory of 'the extended order' is quite as much an ideological and culture-bound theory as those of Marx – and it should be noted, is equally deterministic.

To have the philosophy and practice of the Right claiming total truth over against the philosophy of the Left is a desperate and fantasy-filled travesty which gives Marx the victory by opposing him with a mirror image ideology. As we approach the twenty-first century we must turn our backs on this nineteenth-century polarisation which claims that its dichotomies (Socialism versus Capitalism) exhaust the possibilities of reality, history and humanity. To approach the twenty-first century with nostalgic longing for Victorian values or obsolescent concern with Victorian controversies is to confess that we have no future and that those of us who can, should eat, drink and be merry for tomorrow we die. (Despite the fact that it is not obviously evident that increased consumption increases happiness. Obese victims of heart disease or lean victims of executive stress are not obviously merry.)

It is all a matter of dilemmas and how you respond to them. A di-lemma arises because there are two premises for understanding or action which conflict or compete. In Greek a 'lemma', among other things, is the premise of an argument. What happens when two premises – which may be equally obvious, or in some ways equally unavoidable – conflict? You are left with an unsolved problem which appears insoluble. You are impaled on the horns of a dilemma. This is generally held to be an uncomfortable and untenable position. So the established response is to wriggle off the horns and demonstrate – come what may and at whatever cost – that one of the two 'lemmas' really dominates both the argument and consequent practices. In short, one of the 'lemmas' is consistent with reality and the other must be discarded. That is the theory. However, who ever said that human reality and experience of the world and of one another must fit together in a sealed system which removes all possibilities of dilemmas and necessity for tentative, provisional and risky explorations? Not Plato or Aristotle, or Confucius or the philosophers of the Tao; certainly not Jesus, nor Buddha, nor Mohammed, not even Kant, Darwin or Einstein. Indeed, if there were such a system then there could be no freedom, unless you redefine freedom almost beyond recognition as 'freedom is the acceptance of necessity', as it seems some Marxists and some Marketeers are wont to do. My gut reason for opposing this sleight of hand is that the proponents of such theories always seem to argue that this means that everyone must accept their version of how the theory works out and mysteriously the theory always seems to work out to promote their particular power and interest. I am not entirely sure philosophically what is the weight to ideological suspicion but I am pretty sure that as a human being I suspect people who use necessity in their favour.

I would suggest that freedom is a matter of dilemmas and it is of the essence of freedom that dilemmas cannot be eliminated. To my mind this is one of the clearest indications that being human somehow or other involves one in a mystery which is far more exciting than the definition of *homo sapiens* as *homo consumens*.

Socialism may be a fatal conceit as Hayek believes, but the Market system, both environmentally and socially, looks like a fatal mistake. To be human is to work out together what to do now for the sake of our common future. Humanity cannot be defined by theories, and idolatry – whether it be faith in the Market or Socialist idolatry of the State – is never enough.

Capitalism has its own severe and undeniable problems, just as Socialism's undeniable problems have been proved in its collapse across Eastern Europe. Neither has proved the magic solution to the problems of human sin. We need to get back to rethinking fundamental questions of society, of living together and the nature of real flourishing. What sort of wealth is it that contributes to life, liberty and the pursuit of happiness for all?

Present pressures demand new thinking – not just tinkering about but real, hard, new thinking directed towards the development of a new politics and new economics based on principles of community, consensus, and the equal worth of all individual persons. We have to go beyond the idolatry of the Market without turning back to the idolatry of the State. We have to gather together the faith and hope to dream again. As the prophet Joel has God say: 'I will pour out my Spirit upon all flesh and your sons and your daughters shall prophesy, and your young men shall see visions, and your old men shall dream dreams' (Acts 2:17).

The Conservative dream of an enterprise culture with eventual wealth for all, and the Socialist dream of a disciplined community wherein all share with justice and contribute with enthusiasm, have both come up against the limitations of the resources of the world and the limitations of human nature. When treated as isolated sources of dogmatic politics they are not only impracticable, but idolatrous, divisive and destructive. Nevertheless, as human longings contributing to a common community they resonate with deep possibilities and hopes. It is the Christian belief that these longings are a reflection of a real hope and promise of the One True God.

The faith of Christians is that there is a transcendent Worth which puts the selfish interests of human beings in perspective and is able to contribute to the practical combining of dreams and mutual interweaving of political styles which are at present dangerously polarised and over-absolutised. The Christian Church is set up to witness to God's project for a new unity of humankind and to stand for the belief that there is hope of a common community and a common flourishing. We know there is hope, therefore we not only must rethink, but we know that it is reasonable to expect to find other ways. The facts are proving our present paths to be leading over cliffs of self-destruction. It is urgent that we rethink both our politics and our economics and also the meaning of our shared commonwealth. There are alternatives and we must look for them. Simple faith in the God of whom I have been trying to share glimpses simply cannot give up hope, or the worth of people – each individually and all together. But it is difficult, nowadays, to get people to listen to talk about God as God, for debate and interest are nearly always confined to a side issue called 'religion'.

9

Conjuring Tricks with Bones –

Media Illusions as Reality

◆

Looking back over the public controversy of the last six years, I suspect that underlying it all was a conflict of world views. Confusion multiplied as I was interpreted by critics who operated within a different definition of what was illusion and what was 'facing reality'. On the one hand you had the voice of the Spirit of the Age, ably articulated by the media. In this perspective reality is constructed around what can be measured and calculated – what are termed 'hard facts'. In this 'real world' the realm outside that of 'hard facts' is merely that of emotion and conviction – perfectly fine to indulge in but all equally debatable, unprovable and in 'real world' terms, personal and confined to the individual. In turning the spotlight on the Church, this cynicism came up against the world view of faith in God. Faith in God brings a perception of reality overarched by a transcendent purpose; an understanding in which the complex and the mysterious have quite as much place as the two-dimensionally limited realm of 'hard facts'. This is a view of life in which learning to live with, and learn from, not knowing is as important as knowing, for in this struggle lies the essence of being human (rather than being just an animal or some sort of mechanical being – a particularly complex, flesh and blood computer).

In becoming news, I was placed in the context of a world where God, more often than not, is regarded as an anti-social topic. I found that for most journalists, talking about God is something just not done in mixed company. In the mass media world it seems – somewhat like train spotting or bird watching – religion and God are the stuff of early morning or afternoon television and the outer reaches of late night programming, where serious and boring folk sit in empty studios speaking with great sincerity about such worthy topics as Belief, Morality or Prayer. In this world religion is for Enthusiasts. I often sensed in my conversations with journalists an echo of that eighteenth-century Bishop who is recorded as saying to John Wesley, 'Enthusiasm, sir, is a very horrid thing.'

My first stark realisation of the importance of this gulf beween world views came during my introduction to current affairs press conferences in the library at Auckland Castle, after my enthronement service in Durham Cathedral in September 1984. As the meeting progressed, I noticed an interesting phenomenon. So long as I responded dutifully to questions about the miners' strike, Government policy, whether I was made welcome in my new diocese, what I ate for breakfast – the pencils scribbled industriously. But mention God, an uncomfortable hush descended and I faced a room full of fixed expressions of slightly aggressive discomfort. They certainly had not come all this way to hear a bishop preach the Gospel.

From my point of view I was speaking from faith. I was trying to draw attention to the truth about people and about God – but my reality was not of interest. I was news and I faced questioners who were confined by strong conventions as to what was news – so, whatever I said, they picked out those parts of what I was saying that suited their fixed notions. A Jewish friend told me a joke about this to cheer me up at the height of one of the media storms in the early days of my appointment. It went something like this. A Bishop and a Chief Rabbi are in a boat on the Sea of Galilee. A wind comes up and blows the Chief Rabbi's skull-cap into the water. The Bishop gets out of the boat, walks over, collects the cap and, walking back to the boat, returns it to its owner. The next day the headlines read :'Bishop cannot swim'.

In analysing the 'Durham Affair' from the perspective of the thousands of letters sent to me over the years, I think it is fair to say that every 'controversy' can trace its origins back to the particular slant given by the daily press to its coverage of what I was saying and how I said it. It was newspaper headline summaries of full-length television and radio programmes, multi-page speeches and sermons, that produced misleading abbreviations such as 'Doubting Bishop', 'God is a Woman', 'the Resurrection: a conjuring trick with bones'.

The postbag I have collected over the past six years highlights a need to examine media assumptions about reality and how they shape public perceptions. The attitudes displayed by many of the letters raise both interesting and worrying questions about the relationship between our mass-media as the principal source of information about the world around us, and the possibility of proper public debate of matters of deep human, or simply common, concern.

All branches of the news media, whether radio, press or television, share certain conventions. Firstly, all current affairs journalists work increasingly within the limitations of a 'thirty second' culture which demands that every argument be rendered down into its most simplistic and clear-cut components. Secondly, they work under the broad convention that news deals with matters of conflict and the unexpected.

Under the pressure of these conventions reality is commonly squeezed into something approximating black and white terms – on the one hand this, on the other that. Witness, for instance, the time when a local journalist picked up an article I had written for the Durham Diocesan magazine about the way we think about God. In it, I expressed sympathy for those who find the pronoun 'he' too limiting – for God is beyond gender. I had no very useful solution to this problem, having got no further than the clumsy and inadequate occasional substitution of He/She/It. This wrestling was fed into the national news network along the lines of 'God is Woman, says Bishop'. The logic appeared to be that if 'he' was inadequate then the only alternative must be 'she'. (Although I suspect the main reason for the inaccuracy was that it made a good headline. 'God beyond Gender' hardly has the same punch.)

News providers operate in a harsh world of audience ratings

and circulation figures. There is the ever-present pressure not merely to catch the attention and inform, but also to keep the audience's attention by entertaining. Thus the chosen reality must not only be reported but dramatised for maximum effect. Take, for instance, a classic introduction to a television programme in which I was asked to face the questions of a group of young people in late 1984. I was introduced like this:

In the approach to Christmas he has reasserted his belief that the Virgin Birth was no more than a myth and he even denies the story of the Resurrection of Christ. His consecration in July as Bishop of Durham, the fourth most senior office in the Church of England, brought howls of protest from many practising Anglicans. One cleric resigned, others said his views fell little short of heresy. Fourteen thousand signed a petition calling for reconsideration of his enthronement at York Minster. And when fire destroyed the roof of the Minster two days later there were those who claimed it was divine retribution. In a few short months he has become the most controversial churchman in Britain today.

I could challenge the accuracy of these lines on several points. For instance, I could say that the use of 'no more than a myth' debases the word 'myth' to the level of fairy-tale, whereas myths have long played an honourable role in faith. 'He even denies the story of the Resurrection' is misleading, implying the denial of the Resurrection itself, which is the opposite of what I preach. The petition referred to was reported at the time to be of around 10 000 signatures, although the fact that a significant number of them had been gathered from choirboys and other schoolchildren was never highlighted. Its aim was to postpone my consecration as bishop, not enthronement as Bishop of Durham (they are two separate ceremonies). As for the inevitable mention of the York Minster fire, it is always interesting what journalists choose to give emphasis to. Some time after the York fire, the main tent at a fundamentalist rally in Keswick was struck by lightning and burnt to the ground – yet this occurrence was hardly reported. Perhaps evidence of divine schizophrenia just did not suit the journalists' idea of appropriate godly behaviour.

These 'facts' might have been put in an introduction but they never were. Such qualifications just would not suit such a controversial and infamous character as the 'unbelieving Bishop'. Talk of Incarnation, hints as to the subtleties of the meaning of myth – such things are just too complicated and the language too specialised for family viewing. The programme which included the introduction above was, on the whole, a very successful one and not in any way deliberately antagonistic to me. It was simply following the common media expectation that the public is not interested in turning on in any numbers to listen to a bishop behaving as a bishop is expected to behave. It is only if he is said to be denying what he is expected to defend, that he is sufficiently interesting to be worthy of mainstream attention.

It has often been put to me that I am too negative about my presentation of the Gospel. Why am I such a 'doubting' bishop? The short answer is probably because 'enquiring' has too many letters for the copy-writers and lacks the desired punch for a good headline. The matter of my public image as someone who is always raising difficulties about belief rather than affirming it, arose in many ways from the way the news media works. It was my experience that journalists tended to pick up what looked like the negative element in a statement, leaving out the argument of which it was part. Witness the misquotation of the Resurrection being *much more than* a conjuring trick with bones. The reason for using the phrase in its original context of a Radio 3 discussion programme was in an effort to get across that we were not talking about something as dry and boring as the resuscitation of a corpse. I went on to say that the glory of the Resurrection is that it is the raising up of Jesus transformed – though still in the wholeness and completeness of his person – so he is alive for evermore. I personally think this was a clear affirmation of the Gospel, but it was not reported.

Once I was elected a news item, I found it became more or less impossible to avoid complying with the tag of 'controversial' as the demands of the media constantly put me into adversarial settings. The whole process of turning a comment into a story was structured to present the most clear-cut demonstration possible of 'in the blue corner X and in the red corner Y'. One of my fonder memories is of a time I was called into the studios of a prestigious television news show to defend my position opposite a fellow bishop who was mistakenly imagined by the researchers to be a fierce personal opponent. The face of the researcher when we hailed each other in a friendly fashion was a delight. As there happened to be only ten minutes or so to go before airtime there was nothing to be done and the producer had to put up with the uninspiring sight of two bishops having a civilised theological discussion. We enjoyed ourselves and I received several thoughtful letters as a result of the broadcast, but it just was not 'news'.

I was intrigued to discover, during my various turns with the media circus, how haphazard is the process by which you find yourself reported. Coverage depends on so many factors – whether the wire services used by the major media operators pick up an event or whether there is a local contact or stringer around to turn it into a story to feed to a national newspaper. Finding yourself on the six o'clock bulletin also depends a lot on what other news is about at the time. After the first furore in 1984, every Easter journalists would make a pilgrimage to Durham and turn up enquiring charmingly about my sermon. Whatever I said, however orthodox, there tended to be a certain amount of coverage. Some, often political, person would be found to give suitable colour to the story with appropriate expressions of outrage or opposition and a certain amount of ink would be spilt. By 1989 I fondly hoped that all parties would have tired of this game. That year – in common with many of my fellow bishops – I accepted the invitation of my local television station to be interviewed for their late night religious magazine programme to be broadcast on Easter Day (although, as with many low budget programmes, it was pre-recorded several weeks in advance). The interview was supposed to take a fairly meditative tone – part of a thoughtful half-hour for church-goers to mark the end of an important religious festival. That was the intention. Now the run-up to Easter weekend 1989 proved to be singularly lacking in news. So it happened that the press release drawn up by some bright spark in the television station's publicity department failed to end up in its rightful place in the bin. The story was so tired by now that even professional opponents found it hard to muster the old vim and vigour of condemnation. In order to give some semblance of a new twist, the line chosen was that not only was the Bishop reiterating old doubts on the major Christian festival, but that his timing was particularly tasteless as the story broke on the Saturday, thus spoiling some people's enjoyment of Easter Day. The truth of the matter was that there would have been no fuss but for the dearth of news and the desperation of editors attempting to fill their pages. So once again the Bishop of Durham disturbed the calm of the Easter weekend and the office answerphone did sterling service. I was booked to encounter three television crews on the lawn after my Sunday service when reprieve came from a rather unhappy source. A gunman had run amuck in a nearby town. The journalists went off after a real story and I was left in peace.

The gap between reality as lived and experienced by living human beings, and the sharply focused snapshots presented by news reports is considerable. The process of reporting incidents and issues as news inevitably dramatises them. On the television screen and 'written up' in articles, human beings all too easily become 'personalities', clear-cut caricatures of humanity, not the complex flesh and blood creatures we all know ourselves to be. My six years as a 'personality' have underlined for me how important it is that we should all be clear how we regard our current affairs news media.

In many ways the coverage I experienced, along with the ability to gauge in some way public reaction to that coverage in the correspondence I received, revealed a public desire to consume news and debate presented as entertainment, while often responding to it as if it were simple information. Hence, the caricature of the 'Infamous Bishop of Durham', lampooned in the popular tabloid press, was treated by many correspondents as the real David Jenkins, Bishop of Durham. It was worrying to see how eager certain members of the public were to accept the ill-informed and uncontextualised versions of the debate fed to them by their newspapers. Of even greater concern was the apparent willingness of many to be seduced into adopting the exaggerated language of soap-opera emotions so skilfully encouraged by much of the media. Above all, it was the raising of the pitch of the debates to a wildly emotional level which at points made rational argument, exposition or explanation impossible.

The issues raised by my experience were not just a question of the responsibility of the media and whether they should have kept better standards, but also the naïveté of the public that they could have been so easily manipulated. The question arises of how far we are all, as audiences, partly responsible for that manipulation by our own ranking of entertainment above information and debate.

During the high years of the controversy, an awful lot of anger and moral indignation was flung about through the prompting of press coverage. Emotion ran highest in the tabloid press. Time and time again, the most virulent commentators were journalists who, though not practising Christians themselves, felt they had pertinent contributions to make. Yet by what authority did they shape the debates? Particularly in the coverage of doctrinal issues (such as the debate over the interpretation of the Virgin Birth story) reporting of the 'Durham Affair' between 1984 and 1988 (apart from that of certain specialist journalists working mainly for the religious press and broadcasting) revealed just how singularly ill-informed about the Christian religion are the mass of our country's journalists.

Throughout, the reporting was dogged by journalists setting false contexts for the debates that were taking place within the Church (in the process shaping a wider 'controversy' as some Christian observers took offence at exaggerated reports of division and distress among the faithful). Struts in the structure of faith were regularly picked on and promoted to the status of foundations, while civilised debates about detailed interpretations of commonly held doctrines were magnified into heresy and schism – as in the case of the Virgin Birth debate. The story of the virgin birth of Jesus is not a basic tenet of the Christian faith. The basic tenet the story is conveying is that there is some fundamental sense in which God was so involved, not only in the birth of Jesus, but in the person of Jesus, that there is a real sense in which Jesus is the Son of God. The shorthand for this fundamental Christian doctrine is the Incarnation. Theological ignorance was perfectly understandable for secular journalists switching from the latest parliamentary story to plunge into the depths of religious controversy, but, given the gusto with which the press entered into the debate, there could have been a little more research done. As a bishop and a Christian it was somewhat frustrating to be called to account by members of the public for charges of heresy made by commentators who could not even distinguish between the Incarnation and the Immaculate Conception (the latter refers to the conception of the Virgin Mary, not Jesus).

It was equally frustrating (although at the same time enlightening) to have experience of being widely misquoted in the press and then attempting to get that misquotation corrected. I found that once reports come to be printed and are put 'on file' it is almost impossible to get the impression of their verdict eradicated. For one thing your media tag has been established. In my case I was 'the doubting bishop'. To suddenly rewrite me as 'the believing bishop', quite apart from being perfectly unexceptional and therefore un-newsworthy, would also confuse everybody. The repeated recycling of old misrepresentations seemed partly to be a result of the way research is carried out. I found that most researchers (in press, television and radio) place heavy reliance on looking up past articles. The same articles which have carried the previous misquotations. It is surprising, too, how many people, telephoned by journalists for their comments, rely on what has been printed in the papers for their assessment of what has actually been said. So the merry-go-round continues and articles go on being printed carrying authoritative sounding phrases such as: 'On the religious programme *Credo* the Bishop designate said that three of the miracles in the Bible – the Virgin Birth, the walk on water and the Resurrection were probably invented by early Christians.'

It has been hard to avoid the conclusion that, in reporting the

'Durham Affair', the news media were not, for the most part, interested in the argument but the scandal. Once the scandal faded the mass media were no longer interested and it was against the nature of the medium to correct misinformation with regard to old stories. This is not to attribute malice to the journalists but rather to point out the limitations of present news conventions.

From my earliest days I forged my belief under the ethos of a traditional liberal, critical education which maintained that if you really cared about something, you criticised it, analysed it, wrestled with it, and took it apart so that you might understand and be as clear as possible about what you believed. The furore that surrounded the early years of my appointment seemed to say that this way of critical analytical thinking was now to be ruled out of order as inappropriate for a bishop. This was a deeply troubling challenge, not only to myself, but also to my understanding that the application of critical thought is an essential part of fulfilling the potential of individual persons created in God's image.

On a personal level, at first I imagined that all the abuse was not affecting me. My critical and academic training led me to believe that I could distance myself from the feelings of anger and hurt that any human being must feel when they see some odd distortion of themselves set up as a public Aunt Sally. In my first few months in the appointment I found myself struggling with some pretty black feelings of depression, until one day, walking in the park at Bishop Auckland, I recognised just how very angry I was. Once I faced the conceit of supposing that I could avoid or control such basic human responses, the cloud lifted. However, deep down I still carry a lasting legacy from those darkish days. What affected me most, I think, was the shock of finding that some Christians were so quick to condemn on the basis of trivialising and uninformed reports carried by tabloid sections of the secular press rather than trust a fellow Christian to be – at the very least – trying to live honestly out of faith. On balance, trial by public opinion served a useful purpose. Under journalistic fire I was forced to hone precisely what I really believed. Under such conditions you have to be sure that you believe whatever it is you stand up for, deeply enough to be prepared to be hounded for it.

Oddly enough, looking back, I have no regrets about what I have said or the way it was taken up. I have enjoyed many of the fascinating conversations and encounters with journalists and others that the whole public side of the controversies occasioned. I may have found certain aspects of the fuss tedious, but the whole business of trying to get people to think again about how God is present today, and how that spills over into society today, is a wholly exciting and worthwhile thing. I can honestly say I have come through the last six years without any feelings of ill-will towards the journalistic profession. It remains the case that in interviews I still see a human being asking a question, not a representative of untrustworthy or threatening media. It is possible that this attitude has got me into trouble on occasions, but I remain convinced that the risk is always worth taking.

I do not believe that Christianity can afford to shun the media. Press, radio and television permeate the majority of our lives – providing a major part of our entertainment and dominating our sources of information. It is important that opportunities are taken to plant a flag, as it were, to signal that the Church is concerned with the real world and things that matter to ordinary human beings. It is a good thing for a bishop to turn up in unexpected places in order to remind people that the Christian faith is for everybody and about everything. This does not mean that taking such opportunities does not have its dangers – I am sure I made mistakes, anyone would under those conditions – but if you are really caught up by the truth of something, you cannot afford to be silenced by the possibility that you might be misunderstood. Controversy arose as I pursued a certain line of spiritual enquiry. Although my purpose as a bishop certainly does not include being a rent-a-quote to the media (and I have never given in to that pressure from journalists), it was clear to me from the beginning that I should confront any question that came up that impinged on what I was dealing with, with the maximum straightforwardness and honesty in regard for the truth – not only as it was seen within the Church but as it might be seen from outside.

One of the great dangers we are faced with at the moment is that of fantasy, not only in media manipulation but in politics and political parties which are failing to face the deeper questions about people, how they suffer and how they live; about the way the world is and how careful we have to be about the way we use it and our neighbours. It is imperative that men and women come to terms with the fact that the central truth about reality is that there is always more to it than you think. A major challenge of our times is that the technical and entertainment demands of our mass media encourage us to think less and less while inviting us simply to react and adopt sloganised convictions.

Although I have tried in my dealings with the media to come to terms with the convention that the average attention span of the average inhabitant of the Western living room lasts approximately half a minute, I personally find it very hard to accept. Such limitations are entirely contrary to my natural approach to life. At heart I remain an academic who considers it important to think – although I realise this is not always easy. A student of mine once came to me in confusion about some lectures I was giving on the doctrine of God. I started explaining that what we were doing was trying to think about how people think about God. I encountered a gaze of utter bewilderment and elicited the confession: 'Yes, professor, but you see – I have difficulty thinking.' I do not think this is a rare problem. In the present climate there seems to be a premium against thinking. Over the last six years I have had a whole range of abusive epithets flung at me, but perhaps the most worrying position I have faced is the adoption of the line: 'I am a bear of little brain and no match for your great intellect, so I shall not argue, I shall just tell you that you are wrong.'

The reduction of human debates to simplistic assumptions and dogmatic assertions of truth is tyrannous and destructive of humanity, human community and human neighbourliness. If belief in God teaches you anything, it teaches that reality is complex and human beings gain in their humanity by striving and searching for meaning beyond superficial and simplistic judgements.

Sometimes I am accused of denying the obvious. This statistic *proves* that things are improving. *We all know*. But do we? One of the things I find as a theologian and a preacher is that about as many people believe the incredible as doubt the indubitable. Reality is never as one-dimensional; as any set of statistics or facts. As rational creatures with the power of thought, we have to question the choice of models or perspectives within which we locate what are declared to be facts. Let me give an illustration. One of the things that struck me from my first year in the House of Lords was that Bills that were represented as being in the interests of freedom of the individual had approximately one clause about freedom and eighty-odd clauses about regulation. This was particularly true about the Transport Bill of 1985 and the Health Bill of 1989. The sort of freedom they were concerned with, in short, assumed the necessity of an awful lot of regulation.

Faith and ideology affect the way we see things and the perspectives within which we both select 'facts' and arrange them. It is not enough to follow the 'we all know this' syndrome and cease to analyse, merely because of the current dominating assumption. To bow to theoretical perceptions as givens is to return to the old tyrannical model of the King knows (assisted by the priest), and the rest of us must just toe the line.

I suspect that widespread familiarity with television and photography has encouraged a fundamental shift in the way we perceive reality. It is so easy to look at a piece of film and imagine we see 'what really happened'. But with all our amazing technological skills and discoveries we still have not managed to demystify reality. It remains complex, multi-faceted and impossible to encompass in any absolute or final way. Portrait photographers can produce excellent likenesses which, nonetheless, will only capture one aspect of a person, while others – though highly skilled professionals – can produce portraits which friends of the sitter will find almost unrecognisable. (Let me pass on a few tips – never allow a portrait to be taken with a fish-eye lens. Back lighting is a mistake – it can transform the most benign countenance into a face that would be at home in a horror film – and if you find a photographer inclined to crouch at your feet, it is not a sign of respect. Whatever he or she says about artistic licence, be warned that what will strike the viewer of the final picture will be your complacent double chins and the supercilious way you have of looking down your nose at people.) Any human communication is inevitably 'written up' in the light of individual perceptions and conditioned by the technical circumstances of the means used to convey it. Television interviews – as with radio or written reports – are generally cut (and if uncut, will be strictly recorded to a certain length of time). You may appear to the viewer to be responding to the question of another interviewee when you have never even met the person in the previous shot, and you were actually answering a completely different question – only the producers neglected to inform you as to how they intended to use your contribution. The process of news reporting inevitably involves value judgements as to what is the story, what are the facts, and what will interest people.

A foreign correspondent once told me a story about working in Beirut in the early eighties. The journalists tended to patronise one central hotel and the fighting around them was such they scarcely had to venture out to get first-hand reports of the struggle on the streets as it surged around and even entered the hotel bar on occasion. Then a new crew arrived for a particular American news service. The producer, looking to make his name, decided to strike out on his own and get a new perspective on 'the reality of a city in conflict' away from the pack. He moved his crew to another hotel further down the coast. They were back within the week. Not a single gun battle or militia man had come their way. Although we are right to admire the courage and dedication of our news men and women, risking at times great danger and discomfort to bring back reports from around the world, it is useful to remember that one instance of violence makes a 'story' in a way that millions of peaceful lives just do not.

I am not advocating complete distrust of the media. Indeed I am convinced that responsible reporting and a free press are vital to a civilised and democratic society, but it is important that the public be sophisticated enough to keep in mind the conditioning factors of the medium. Particularly there is urgent need to resist the media-generated notion that unless something can be summarised in fifteen seconds or in a headline it cannot be interesting or contain important truths. We have to build up enough confidence and faith to wrestle with the complexities of life. There is great danger in tidying everything up, so that there are no ambiguities, no rough edges, no two ways of seeing things that must not inevitably engage in a battle where only one can emerge supreme. It is a misapprehension of reality, and ultimately destructive, to expect to find at the heart of every matter a simple, clearly defined reality that all right-minded folk must come to agree with once they understand it.

One of the odd and interesting things I have been led to reflect upon in recent times is the fact that the adjective 'controversial' has come to be held as something of a pejorative adjective. This seems to me to be very odd. Where did we lose the notion that having a good argument to try and shake out the truth of the matter is something worthwhile? The way to treat an opponent with whom you disagree is to respect him or her, and seek to controvert them. They will try and controvert back, and out of the whole process some truth will emerge that will be greater than either party. It is sad how so many people seem to have lost their nerve about having a really good wrestle about the truth. I do not see why citizens who care about something they share in common cannot have controversial conversations. Without such arguments, such thrashing out of problems, there is no hope of getting through to a common consensus about the way forward. Proper civilised argument, carried on by rational people open to new information and insights, brings people together over common concerns. It is the aggressive sloganising of closed minds which leads to conflict and destruction.

Our times appear to be marked by far too much ideology and not nearly enough observation and rigorous thought. Real questions cannot be dismissed. Taken too far, that way leads to barbarism and fascism. Dogmatism – and particularly dogmatism when it is expressed in the exercise of power – threatens the reasoned discourse and genuinely exploratory enquiry which is essential both to accountable democracy and to any humane and realistic development of pragmatic politics. I believe it is appropriate to introduce a suggestion of thuggery here, for too often we see counter-arguments or assemblages of evidence simply bludgeoned into oblivion. Miners going through the agony of the end of a way of life are branded hooligans and anarchists; street protesters against an unpopular Government policy are labelled criminals where possible, or easily manipulated and misled if not. Every day we can see examples of the increasing habit in political interviews for politicians to expend more energy flatly rejecting opposing arguments and denigrating those who pose them, than in engaging in debate and arguing their case. The present parlous state of domestic politics whereby parties slang one another about policies is an abomination. Argument must go forward. Somebody has got to think about what to do next rather than expend all their energy on explaining that 'opponents' are not doing very well. We are all doing badly and we all have a common interest in finding a way forward through our controversies.

Everything is always dependent on judgement of facts, judgements about the way things really are, and judgements about how things might develop. All political and all social affairs are necessarily full of deep and potentially disastrous ambiguities. Human beings can never be completely right, either in their appreciation of facts or in their application of decisions or programmes. Those who behave as if they think they are, are being thuggish with respect to those who disagree with them, and this thuggery constitutes a grave threat to both freedom and to that reasoned and exploratory approach which is required by difficult and complex matters.

Those readers who have followed me through this book will probably have gathered by now that two of my great loves are the Ancient World and the origins of words. Bear with me while I indulge both loves, for I believe the Greek origins of our word for, and concept of, 'community' and 'private' are enlightening. Although our present society is far from similar to that of the Ancient Greeks, they did do some pretty clear thinking about the knotty problem of how men and women can best live together in society.

The Greek for 'common' is 'koinos' and the Greek for both

'one's own' and 'private' is 'idios'. So 'koinos' refers to the common which makes up 'koin-onia', which is the Greek for 'community' and 'togetherness', and 'idios' refers to the private or one's own. Originally what was 'common' or 'koinos' went with public duties and opportunities as a citizen, while what was private or 'idios' went with one's own private affairs. As time went by, some people among the citizens who stayed on the private side of things – the sort of person who is not 'politikos' – began to be known as 'idiotikos'. That means that they were not concerned with the polis (the city) but simply with their private selves. Hence a private citizen was one who took no part in public affairs. Now people who stayed out of things also became ignorant of them and incompetent at them. So 'idiotikos' came to mean 'lay' (not an expert), 'ignorant' and 'not knowing what is going on'. Thus as time and usage went on, 'idiotikos' went from being a private citizen to being an 'idiot'. That is to say 'idiotic' – incompetently shut up in one's own private, limited ways. In short, to be so private and concerned with what is one's own is simply to be an idiot.

It seems that we have reached a stage in our own society where the idiotikos are in danger of outnumbering the politikos – and indeed we are encouraged by our mass media to be idiotikos rather than politikos to such effect that our politics and democracy are ailing.

Until the public faces up to the layers of influences which go into the final printed or broadcasted report, democracy and informed debate are severely threatened. There is a need to cultivate perspective and alternative sources of information in contrast to present increasing reliance on mass-media sources. It is possible for individuals to resist the pressure to be turned into idiotikos and reassert their right to be politikos.

What separates the idiotikos from the politikos is information. We all need broad information about what is going on in our society and the world around us, so that as individual, responsible members of our society we can make reasonably informed judgements about matters of common, public concern. Without such a basis, democracy is but window-dressing for the manipulation of the mob by whoever has the money, the wit or dominance of the political machinery of the State. If free-dom and democracy are valued, then individual citizens cannot shuffle off the responsibility of thinking and judging for them-selves on to anyone, any party or any theory – however appar-ently pure the individual, powerful the party or authoritative the theory. In the past few years I have been told off by certain people who say that I wish to take too much authority onto myself – that I try to dictate to elected governments. At the same time, in other areas deemed proper spheres for Church influ-ence, such as individual morality, I am accused of not being authoritative and dictatorial enough. I would say that both accu-sations are misplaced. My job as a Christian and as a citizen is to make a contribution to a common task. So many people want speakers or 'authorities' to do their thinking for them, and take their responsibility from them. However, if politics and democ-racy – and indeed morality – are to flourish, we have to be clear about the need for common commitment and participation.

Aristotle said that making a judgement always involves having a perception. The essence of judgement lies in how you perceive a thing. The only means you have of checking your perception is in being as well informed as you can manage and to be concerned to understand rather than just be right. For instance, reading the original material 'reported on' in news items and comment columns is clearly impractical for most of us, most of the time, but individuals can be wary of reports which present matters and people in black and white terms. An informed public, interested in public debate, is the soundest basis for responsible and free press and broadcasting.

There is a serious problem in our society today about how we can get a realistic and trusting debate about the facts of the case under discussion. This is a by-product of conviction politics. It is not a particularly healthy sign when a common political quip is that real statistics are the ones which support 'our' case and fudged, or mistaken, statistics are the ones which argue against it. There is urgent necessity for patient investigation of particu-lar problem areas, careful documentation and presentation by publication by pressure groups, academics, and professional groups. There is a need for dependable statistics and information by which to assess the 'truth' of situations. Only by building up and making public a body of information which is commonly accepted as dependable can we start recreating a broadly trusted 'common ground' on which rational argument (aimed towards broad consensus) can re-emerge as the basis of a way forward through our dilemmas. There is a constant need for publicity. No one must be allowed to fancy that they know beyond a shadow of a doubt what is what. People in power and people who vote need to be better informed about their society and what 'is actually going on'.

Diverse groups hold together firstly, because they have a common interest in sheer survival and secondly, because they practise politics. Not because they agree about fundamentals or some such concept too vague, too personal and too divine ever to do the job of politics for it. The moral consensus of a free state is not something mysteriously prior to, or above, politics itself. Living together in a society with hope for the future requires open-mindedness on the basis of being human together – not as an option or a luxury for a few educated mavericks, but of necessity.

The present bankruptcy of our politics is evidence of the rather overshot, under-committed, bored and tawdry state we are now in. The two mirror images of the world (Market Capitalism and State Socialism), which continue in ghostly form to dominate such limited political thinking as there is, seem to have mesmerised all those who find such world views unconvincing and hopeless. The sterile deadlock of our politics is driving more and more people towards the view that politics are hopeless. It is statistically the case that only 45 per cent of the people who bothered to vote in the last election, voted for the prospectus of the present Government. Much of the population is increasingly frustrated. In some the response is to take refuge in apathy. I am haunted by a vivid memory of a photograph carried by some daily papers during the 1987 election. It was of a down-at-heel youth, in a desolate urban landscape, walking past a wall on which the graffiti read 'if voting changed anything they would have made it illegal'. A snapshot of reality that contains unpleasant implications and one which I have found echoed on many estates and among many people in my own diocese. Others eschew politics and invest their energies in some single issue which is identified as a means of expressing commitment to broad concerns of mankind – ecological and peace pressure groups; attendance at pop concerts to express solidarity with oppressed peoples of South Africa or to raise money for victims of famine. Pressure groups and their concern are laudable, vital even, but they are not enough, while attendance at pop concerts and the purchase of a T-shirt or two reduces the expression of human concern to the level of an act of consumption. Politics is still practised and remains the mechanism of power in our society. The fragmentation of organised opposition to the party in power has grave consequences.

Power unlimited by other perspectives, unchallenged by effective alternatives, is a very dangerous thing. This is why over the last ten years our politics have been in a mess in this country – because we apparently have no effective opposition. With the lack of an effective alternative you cannot expect an inadequate Government to lose an election, although they may come close to it. In any case, the collapse of a powerful group by default is no solution – for there must be some hopeful alternative to replace it.

There is an urgent need for what I would call collaborative realism. Whatever the perspective from which the questions of the need to reform are being approached, it must be recognised that there are shared problems in solving them which extend more widely than the perspective of any one interested party or group. These shared problems are reflected partly in 'your' realism and partly in 'our' realism.

We have outgrown our present political style. What we are to grow into is not clear but we need to reinstate the importance of facts about the human costs of poverty, about social costs and community costs against the presently dominating role given to ideologically framed aims and theories. The pressures of our world seem to call for a return to pragmatic politics. The present conflictual deadlock, where barren dogmatic statements take the place of constructive debate, must be inadequate to the challenges that face our society.

If we are aiming to find a common vision and common ways of working things out on the ground, then we are faced with tough politics which must be pursued with persistence without allowing ourselves to be divided in the pursuit of our common visions – for we have got to live together whether we like it or not. This means that deciding on a programme and dogmatically bludgeoning it through, whatever the opposition, is out. The only way to achieve a common way forward is to be willing to pay the cost of discussion, persuasion and the laying out of information – the cost of delays and compromises.

There needs to be a letting go of old assumptions and the asking of new questions. The basis of this rethink needs to be focused on the importance of persons. We need a common purpose related to participation, votes and power. People have got to feel they are in on this common purpose and that they can make a difference. Democracy cannot survive where a large number of citizens feel excluded from participation. We need to develop approaches which appeal to those who feel left out, or know that they are never going to be listened to. This involves serious work on the matter of shared costs and a real getting down to the issues of neighbourliness touched on in my previous chapter.

Participation is the key to democracy but this is not just a case of access, it is also a case of responsibility and individual motivation. It is time there was a greater public facing-up to the destructive social effects of the underlying pressures of the materialist society we have constructed. How are we to come to terms with the fact that the cult of individual materialism we cherish, goes hand in hand with the production of idiotikos in a way that militates against the flourishing of participatory democracy so boasted of in the West? We are increasingly a fragmented, individual-based culture. How do we encourage more public debate and common concerns?

Too many of us in this country take it for granted that we live in a democracy – that we have arrived. We have ceased to struggle for our freedoms and our democratic rights. But our sense of security is an illusion. To expect to be spoon-fed, to expect freedom to be guaranteed without effort or personal commitment, is the way to wake up to find yourself under tyranny.

To face what is really going on brings the realisation that we may have to think about propositions which may appear, at first sight, unthinkable. One of the reasons you cannot answer the question can be because you are asking the wrong one. This is an elementary rule of science. It might well be quite an important rule both of the spirit and of life in general.

There is an urgent need to re-examine democratic processes, structures, education, so that the widest number of people may make a contribution in some way to the control of what goes on, fostering the accountability of those who carry it out and the possibility of changing that control. It is only by re-examining and reforming the mechanisms of political involvement that we shall discover the vitally needed third way between the dead-lock of anachronistic politics of Left and Right. What would seem to be required is what you might call rational politics, including some form of proportional representation designed to encourage people to take the various political and interest groupings more seriously. A third way might well lie in trying to work out some connection between democracy and community, rather than some connection between democracy and either the Market or the State. In short, a new politics would seek to sub-ordinate both Market and State to people and community.

The challenge to turn the threats sketched out in these last few chapters into promises is to all of us as citizens. It is about politics engaged in by persons. It is about our way of life and whether we can do anything about it. Perhaps we cannot. As was pointed out by a medical friend of mine, life is, after all, a fatal disease passed on by sexual intercourse. Nevertheless, I am convinced by my faith in, and knowledge of, God that humankind has in it more purpose and more ability to share in and shape its own destiny than we are allowed in the present bread and games world of lotus-eating idiotikos, where our humanity and democratic traditions are rapidly sinking from sight in the backwash of the tide of materialism.

10

Loving God and Living with Sin

◆

Over the last six years I have faced the deepest challenge I have ever experienced to my Christian faith and discipleship. I entered my episcopacy in the conviction that bishops are appointed as representative teachers, leaders of and carers for Christian believers. I assumed that this meant an apostolic calling to lead people forward into an ever-deepening exploratory encounter with God in the midst of the circumstances, promises and threats of life today on the basis of the Tradition so far. I uncovered a vocal body of opinion which held that what I would label 'apostolic pioneering' was not what was expected of me. It was not in the episcopal contract that bishops should help people develop appropriate practices for new circumstances and lead them forward into faith and into the future of God. Bishops were expected to protect believers in the comfort and familiarity of practices they already had, behind the dry and fragile barriers of faith once received.

So my attempts to fulfil my calling and responsibility to be a Christian teacher and leader who communicated, as specifically and practically as he could, what difference Christian believing and worshipping made today, were judged, by certain parts of the Church, to be improper, outrageous and – worst of all – faithless. This experience raised for me what I would call a 'continuing discipleship question'. My bluff had been called. I had to strive at all times to be as clear as possible in my head, my heart, my spirit, as to what Christian faith meant and why. May I add, this was the most liberating and sustaining realisation possible. To take up, at the age of sixty, a job which was centred on ecclesiastical manoeuvring and media posturing would simply not have been worth the candle. To be called to deeper investigation and deeper discipleship, however, is worth a life-time and then some.

The experiences of my episcopacy have helped me to clear away much of the debris obscuring the central discipleship questions. It all boils down to: I am a Christian – what does that mean, and why should that meaning I have found be believable to others?

In facing these questions I have found it worse than useless for various people – claiming to speak on the basis of various authorities (whether they be the Bible, the Church, the Pope or just 'Jesus In My Heart') – to tell me that being a Christian has always meant this or that, and therefore must always mean this or that. This is worse than useless for several reasons, one of which is that simple historical inspection reveals that Christian faith has never (indeed no living faith has ever) kept to any one particular list of *this-es* interpreted in any *that* particular way. This is true especially if you are interested enough to go on to ask: 'What do they mean?' Christians have argued about what is involved in Christian faith, about what it means and why this should be so, at least since the time of Paul's first letter to the Corinthians.

The God of the Jewish and Christian religions, if the biblical patterns and dynamics are to be taken seriously rather than read selectively and quoted piecemeal, is a power, a presence, a promise and a possibility who is to be encountered in, and related to, absolutely everything. God is not the boxed-up God of much religion but the life and hope and promise of all that is, can be or will be. According to the Bible, God is forever having to shatter man-made conceits, illusions and idols in order to get down to reality. It is my conviction that any lively faith in the God who is pointed to in the Bible must express itself, and develop itself, through engaging reality and living with questions. These questions are the pressures of God upon us and indicators of the ways in which we must go if we are to serve Him, our neighbours, and His and our world in creative and hopeful ways. This means you cannot be properly and usefully 'theological' unless you are wrestling with an interaction between at least two perspectives – one coming from practical human perceptions of present reality and one coming from an insight of faith and revelation.

Some people seem to find it difficult to believe that I endeavour to conduct my whole life on simple acts of faith. In fact it is because of my faith that I feel obliged again and again to draw attention to the complexities of life. Faith is no more a matter of simplifying to the level of stupidity or ignorance than it is a matter of fantasising that one has got away with things when one has not. Simple faith is the base from which you can face all the complexities of reality.

All this does not imply a rejection of the Bible. It represents a return to the God of the Bible. God, as portrayed in the Scriptures, is not encountered, presented or looked for only in stories of the past. He works in and through history. Therefore, if the history of the West for 2000 years erodes dogmatic authority on all fronts, secular as well as religious, then it is the business of faith to conclude that God does not intend us to respond to Him and to the light He offers through such authority. If we have any prophetic and biblical faith in God then we must be clear that it is contrary to the will of God to attempt to go back on history. As the shared definition of the two great theologians St Augustine and St Anselm put it, theology is a matter of 'faith seeking understanding'. In this sense, Christianity is a discipleship which is concerned not to go back on what has so far been discovered, but to discover how to go on from it in the light of our glimpses of what it will come to.

The crucial questions which naturally arise from this logic, however, are what is involved in 'engagement with the contemporary' and what are the ways of 'taking the contemporary seriously' which are required and legitimate for Christians? We have to be careful to avoid distorting 'theology' into something we feel to be 'relevant'. If we take absolutely seriously both the theological traditions that have come down to us and the pressures of reality as we now experience them, then engaging the contemporary as a theological task can never be simplistic or 'one way'. 'The contemporary' has to be engaged in a testing way as well as in an accepting way. The crucial question is how we are to go on from what we have so far discovered and what sort of glimpses do we have of 'what it will come to'? (This is picking up Chapter 6 about eschatology, that is thinking about the Kingdom of God and what kind of End God has in mind for us.) The issue is neither 'what we have always done', nor 'what is presently fashionable', but what is likely to be true, humanly helpful and humanly hopeful.

The Christian Faith is basically a conviction about Worth. A worth which is so worthwhile that it is infinitely worth living for, and therefore ultimately and absolutely worth dying for. (Not that any particular Christian – certainly not myself – is up to living that way in one's actual life without the Grace of God.) There is something more important than life itself which gives meaning to it. This Worth is God. God who is the source and end of all worth-ship and the offer of worth beyond all measure. This is the God who is, so to speak, behind and beyond and within the dynamics of biblical Revelation; the God who is as He is in Jesus and the True God who is relevant to any and all Ages – even our own.

We live in a secular age which acknowledges few mysteries. Physics, they say, is busy cracking the code of the universe (although every time they do so, they find they need another code, but that is only fascinating). Biology has solved many of the mysteries of evolution. Psychology maps out characters while sociology plots how people behave in groups. There is no mystery anymore about caring for people – for instance to the point where a relationship is so valuable it might even be worth being crucified for it. There is no mystery about sex. Nothing about entering into deeper loves and passions which might so build up that they are worth it for life. We know where we are. We know what is what. What is needed is to produce wealth – that is to say, cash – and spend it as we wish. Freedom for the individual is the first priority and then we shall flourish as best we may – or, as many of us will flourish as we can, and too bad for all the rest. The nearest thing to paradise on earth is the latest shopping mall and its associated leisure complex. That is what life is about. That is prosperity and wealth.

This appears to be where we are assumed to be. I cannot help asking – frankly, is it believable? What is living really about? Is it honestly worth contemplating if it is centred on consumption and little else? Is being an individual about choosing what 'I' like and nothing more? Could that be worth it, and, practically, is it sustainable? What about the family, what about friends – what about persons staying together in relationships because together they can find something that is so worthwhile that it is actually worth giving up something for it – perhaps giving up everything for it. What about Love? And what about Reason? What about the amazing mystery of the ability of human beings to so grapple with their surroundings that they can now begin to produce statistics about the infinite chance there was of there being just that window of opportunity – between the mathematics, the temperature, and the chemistry – for a molecule to emerge which might give life. All these things may not prove anything, but they are infinitely mysterious.

Then this earth we inhabit – can it really be about raw materials and nothing more? Think about the Amazonian rainforests which poor people are chopping up for their survival and rich people are exploiting for their profit. Consider the incredible number of birds and species and plants found in just that one area of the earth – plants which we are now beginning to find out are biochemically useful if we only have the sense to tumble to their importance before we allow them all to be wiped out. Nearer to home – what about each spring which somehow or other, despite all the rubbish and destruction we spew about us, still causes things to grow and look beautiful? What about – to pick up on a detail – the amazing skills of photography nowadays so that you can watch on television the things that no eye but God's presumably has seen before? The sheer beauty of flying things when you slow the motion down and see every frame one after the other. What about all these mysteries about us?

The more I look at the world and the more I experience relationships with other human beings, the more I am convinced by the Christian understanding that men and women are made in the Image of God.

The extraordinary thing is that we have been able to

understand the mathematics of the universe. The reason we can map out the stars, break genetic codes and have to make up our minds about moral issues, is that there is something about us which resonates with God. That is to say that we should face the claim and the possibility that we are, in fact, not a chance but a creation. We may indeed have emerged out of what God has created, as material atoms which have come together eventually to be persons; persons made for love and therefore in the image of God and able to collaborate with God.

Striving after reality and truth is basically a theological exercise. That is to say, it is to do with seeking to get closer to God and what He requires and offers. So it follows that in the midst of all the confusions and disagreements of our times, one of the main contributions real faith in God and serious theology ought to make is to support the refusal to accept any absolute orthodoxies, any dogmatic acceptance of theories political, economic or psychological which shut up men and women in anything less than God.

This has crucial implications, not only for secular theories and political dogmas, but for many of the so-called 'fundamentalist' expressions of religious fervour. If we are to take the God of the Bible seriously, then we have to face the message of the Scriptures that God is continually having 'a controversy with His people'. That is to say, even His most enthusiastic followers frequently get God's purposes dreadfully wrong while pursuing the best of intentions.

At present we are seeing a rise of fundamentalism across religions. The principal engine of recruitment to this movement revolves around a call to return to rigid moral leadership (perceived as once operating to man's benefit in some hazy 'Past') enforced from central institutions such as 'the Church', in response to disturbing times. We are told that if only proper moral leadership is given and enforced, sinful men and women will be returned to the paths of righteousness – on the way refilling our churches, mosques or synagogues and bringing the nation back to order. Sections of believers adopting this line point to their success and the correctness of their analysis in the intensity of their conviction and the numbers that crowd their meeting places.

The problems with this contention are twofold. Firstly, neither conviction nor even the best of intentions are, of themselves, enough. Many ungodly theories and idols throughout the ages have had pretty strong pulling power and deeply convinced followers. Secondly, the record of sectarian religion in its various forms through the ages – with its sharp demarcations between the righteous believers and the unrighteous unbelievers – denies its own major premise, namely that it is the true worship of the Universal God, who is concerned with Worth and Truth everywhere.

When a person or a class of persons longs for the emergence of clear moral leadership in their society, it seems that the glimpse of what men and women are heading towards is primarily perceived in terms of some sort of order. In view of the complexities and difficulties of producing order among human beings, this frequently leads to a strong desire for some person, group of persons or institution, which will have the authority to stop 'them' doing things of which we disapprove and which frighten, disturb and threaten us. Things are getting out of control, and effective moral leadership would bring them under control; things are flying apart and they need pulling together. The implication is that a righteous society – a reflection of the Kingdom of God, even – is one which is regimented and that flourishing and conformity go hand in hand.

Where does this picture of moral leadership come from? It has its roots, I believe, in a very simple model which goes back at least to the Middle Ages in Europe and is reflected in a French slogan which emerged through the confusions of the Reformation and the Counter-Reformation – that of 'un roi, une foi, une loi' (one king, one faith, one law). In this picture, society is the same thing as the State (that which controls power and by which we are governed) and this State is an organic and living whole, headed by one king. The monarch's authority to rule comes from God, who is the object of the one faith which informs the society. The State, headed by one king and informed by one faith, has one law which regulates problems of status and of rights, and even more importantly, of privileges (because most people's rights in those days were asserting their privileges), and of transgressions within that State and society.

Within such a picture the Church is to be looked to for what we might call 'moral leadership', that is to say authoritative declarations about what we ought to believe and what we ought to do. The implication of this is that conformity in both belief and behaviour is essential to the healthy, organic life of the State and of society. It follows, therefore, that non-conformity – not fitting in – not only disturbs the State and is bad for society, it can also be extended to threaten the individual with hell.

History shows that in practice this picture of authoritarian moral leadership is fatally flawed, if you are ultimately drawn to a God concerned with Worth, Love and Truth. Just consider briefly the pile of evidence which suggests that believing in God is bad for humanity. The history of Christianity is very worrying; it includes the Crusades, the Inquisition and anti-semitism. There has been, and there continues to be, great intra-Christian rivalry often conducted with bad temper, ill-will and violence. Believers, all too frequently, organise to display loyalty to God and the Faith by illiberality, bullying and persecution. Whether in matters of faith, or in matters of morals, religious commitment seems to be an excuse to be nasty to people who are alleged, shall we say, to have queer ideas or follow queer practices. These habits are not confined to Christianity; they are endemic in most religions. Islam rejoices in its Jihads, has quite a record of forcible conversions and shows a pretty ugly face in much of its current revivalism. The ambiguities of the Jews, Zionism and the nation State of Israel are alarmingly obvious. The Intifada is troubling, persistent and miserable. We can see, if we follow the papers, how elderly Rabbis controlling small, deeply committed religious parties, can block the formation of any secular government trying to deal with devastatingly pressing problems of peace and living together constructively. We see religious fanaticism around the world and throughout the centuries feeding political incompetence and multiplying personal misery. Then on top of this there is the nearly overwhelming realisation that the Jews, the Christians and the Muslims all claim to worship the one true and only God, and therefore necessarily the same God, whose alleged heavenly demands are supposed to justify hellish behaviour on earth.

It is hardly surprising that some observers conclude that all this religious self-justification is simply a cover for another form of tribal warfare directed by self-interest. Self-interest in this world conveniently linked to a belief that we (always the 'we' to which *we* belong) are chosen for benefit and privilege, not only in this world but also in the next. Looked at coolly, it is plain that, on the basis of their record so far, religious people and institutions are strong and persistent contributors to the case for atheism.

If you are concerned with a True God, that is one who is the centre and embodiment of Worth and Truth, then all that flows from God must be an expression of Worth and Truth. Unworthy means, particularly those destructive of humanity, can never be justified – indeed claiming such means to be 'in the name of God' is a blasphemy. The reality is that simple demands for moral leadership are neither simple nor simply moral. It may be that some people have a sense that society lacks moral leadership. It may be that this sense of unease and longing reflects something very important about our society and represents a significant challenge to the churches. But whatever the problem, it is positively harmful and indeed immoral to look for a response which takes a form which cannot be had – further, a form which should not be had.

False expectations of absolute and encompassable, unchanging truth are the curse of mankind – as much in politics as in religion. The problem lies not with directive dreams of heaven and what might be (according to Christians these dreams are resonances of God), but rather in attempts to draw up blueprints from those dreams in the form of theories or dogmas, and then to pursue them on earth as if they come direct from God or Truth. Both religious authoritarianism and political authoritarianism are idolatries. One way of identifying idolatries is that they cannot cope with risk and the cost of sin. Only the One True God can do that. In pursuit of idolatries casualties are made of such things as freedom, creativity, imagination and worth – all things which make up individual persons, and are of the essence of what being human is all about.

The choice between authoritarian tyranny and living with questions, freedom and risk, revolves around the problem of how human beings cope with the gap between their dreams of justice and order and the down-to-earth reality of human sin, incompetence and falling short. An examination of the dilemmas of freedom gives an illustration of what I am getting at. The dilemmas of freedom focus around attempts to balance tensions and relationships between the individual and the communal. The problem with the political theories we have developed so far is that neither individualism nor collectivism takes account of the fact that the ideal combination of anarchy and community which would fulfil persons occurs only in heaven. That is true even if there is no heaven. (Heaven either stands for what I believe it stands for – namely, where God is God without interruption and so an existence in which one day most of us may share; or else it stands for Utopia, which, as we all know, is both the place where people do well and that which does not exist but is the necessary aim of social pursuit and progress.)

The point about the ideal combination of anarchy and unity existing only in Heaven is that if the free individual is to be truly free then there must be an element of anarchic freedom in which the individual self is not under any other principle, regulation or set of rules than this free self (therefore authoritarian control is not an option). That is properly described as anarchy and it is one side of the ideal of the free person. You being yourself in the best possible way in which you can be yourself without interruption, distortion or diminution. But that requires the perfect community; that you should be you in such a way that your being you enables me to be me in such a way that that enables you to be you – and it is worth it for both and all of us. The main point is that persons have an individual focus and also a social, communal, relational focus. The question is, how do you develop both of them into a relationship with one another so that they tend not to get in the way of one another but actually mutually promote one another?

Once you accept that the ideal balance between individual and communal interests exists only in heaven, then logic leads to the fact that current incompatibilities and tensions between equally important and equally worth-giving resources or solutions are simply a feature of life. For instance, sometimes you have to have more freedom and less justice, and it is simply untrue to argue that because some measure gives you more freedom it therefore must be more just. Sometimes you have to have less freedom and more justice, and it is simply untrue to say that because something is more just therefore people are more free. You do not solve such practical dilemmas by discounting one side of the equation. Probably the whole of politics and economics is to do with this fact of incompatibility, tension and conflict. This may be a tragedy but it may also be an important opportunity because it may be precisely in these tensions that the whole possibility of free action, living out of the potential of humanity and being part of creation, actually exists.

Neither the march of history nor the destiny of man is heading for an end on earth where the perfect rules produce a perfect society. The arrangement of society so that human beings may live in the most worthwhile sense, so yearned after by religious and political dreamers throughout the ages, has no blueprint. Righteousness cannot be 'achieved' in any 'capture it and preserve it' sense, for being human beings together in the most worthwhile sense is a continual and ever-varying process, not a goal. There is no one adequate and all-embracing theory or dogmatism about the meaning of life, Christianity or history. All we have are experiences to be reflected on, searches to be conducted and considered, practices to be developed, used and revised, theories which are useful up to a point as working models and temporary guiding principles, and intuition about what is involved in being human. No one person, no theory, no dogma, no religion, can pre-empt the future by pretending to possession of blueprints to the City of God, Utopia or simply 'The Truth'.

In Christian theology, heaven is where all relationships are fulfilled. The point about love and relationships is that they are continuous. There is no possibility of reaching an End, in the sense of a static conclusion. (Here we have no abiding City.) That is why Christians talk about pilgrimage – moving ever on into the love of God. Finding out about Worth and Love is an endless process – that is the joy of it and that is why heaven will never be a bore. Therefore, in the context of Christian understanding, aspirations to produce human flourishing in God's name, through authoritarian manipulation of men and women, must be an idolatrous mistake based on a misunderstanding about the meaning of being human and the extent of the ability of sinful man to achieve perfection or Truth on earth.

If the sin of men and women is always going to stand in the way of our achieving our best ideals, can there be any hope of human progress in a 'desirable' direction or are we reduced to being at the mercy of chaos and chance? I am convinced that Christianity is the one theology and faith up to dealing with these problems of sin and risk.

History demonstrates that it is not possible to arrange human society so as to neutralise the effects of sin. Authoritarian attempts to do so have merely resulted in tyranny and more sin. So is there another way? Christianity does present 'another way', but it is not necessarily an easy way.

In the Gospel of Matthew there is a story about Peter, the disciple whose dedication to Jesus earned him the name of 'the Rock'. 'From that time Jesus began to make it clear to his disciples that he had to go to Jerusalem and there to suffer much . . . At this Peter took him by the arm and began to rebuke him: "Heaven forbid!" he said. "No, this shall never happen to you." Jesus turned and said to Peter: "Away with you, satan; you are a stumbling block to me. You think as men think, not as God thinks." ' (Matthew 16:21–23)

What turned the disciple Peter from being a rock of the faith to an adversary of the faith, in the story in Matthew, was his rejection of the Messiah and Lord who was servant, sufferer and sacrifice. In short he was heading for a way of interpreting the faith that denied the faith in the form in which it was to be embodied in Jesus.

Jesus pointed to a God whose Love is so great that it can overcome all sin, but that does not mean that there is some magic formula through which we can avoid sin. If men and women are free agents then sin cannot be discounted. Jesus Christ brought the good news that sin shall not have dominion over us but his example demonstrated that the way of Love and Worth involves suffering. We are offered salvation not solutions – or righteousness – and the way to salvation lies through repentance. As Paul's letter to Philippians 2:5 put it: 'Let this mind be in you, which was also in Christ Jesus: who, being in the form of God, thought it not robbery to be equal with God: But made himself of no reputation, and took upon him the form of a servant, and was made in the likeness of men. And being found in fashion in man, he humbled himself, and became obedient unto death, even the death on the Cross.' This picture of worth achieved through suffering love is not some black twist added to life by some sadistic cultic god, but an essential insight into the true cost of freedom of individual persons who can only be full persons in community.

The illusion of absolute truth accessible to human beings on this earth destroys the concept of an independent God and undermines true freedom. If we are to begin to face the Mystery of God – a Mystery which can encompass the vastness of the universe, the depths of wickedness, the burning intimacies and promises of love and persons, then we must share in the risks of God – risks which include the possibility of suffering, sin and getting things wrong. The power of Love is not having everything cut and dried, with reserve force to push the divine plan through. Such power could leave no room for the freedom which true love requires.

As the price for living as created beings with the responsibility and creative possibilities born of free choice, we have to accept we are not offered easy and right solutions to our dilemmas. The bland, if seductive, sales-pitch of our materialist society that 'there is a solution to every want and desire' is a dangerous and childish illusion. The truth is that human beings cannot avoid suffering or mischance in life. The Christian Good News is that suffering need not be purposeless. Although we all die in the end, death need not be The End – truth, justice, holiness and love are always worth fighting for, and indeed, dying for. Death does not have the last word, for God demonstrated His will and power to keep things going for eventual goodness, love and life by raising Jesus from the dead.

Much of the attraction of authoritarian dogmatisms and idolatries is rooted in our common fear of risk and insecurity. Sinful human beings mostly do not feel up to bearing the god-like burdens of freedom and suffering.If you accept that the way of suffering love is God's way, it is no wonder that He is not popular – the real God that is, not the various fantasies of the religious. The question remains, however, whether following our gut reactions to common fears is in fact the most hopeful and constructive way of dealing with those fears.

Coming to terms with reality means we all have to accept that sometimes we are brought near to despair, finding ourselves lost and frightened. Discovering that you have no answers can be a very disturbing and painful thing. On the other hand it cannot be ignored that history and the world about us demonstrate that it is no solution for men and women to run for the false security of blind faith in some dogmatism or idolatry. It is interesting to note that in the Scriptures you find Wilderness right at the heart of living the biblical faith. Elijah came into the wilderness in order to get his faith renewed and his message corrected. John the Baptist went off into the wilderness to start his mission, dressed just like Elijah. Jesus, after he had been baptised by John the Baptist, went off into the wilderness for his temptation, to work out the meaning of what he was caught up in. In the biblical understanding, lostness can have its positive side. Wilderness brings us away, disturbs us and helps us to rethink and so move on through uncertainty to newness. In the deeply questioning experience of despair, unseen barriers of selfishness and idolatry can be broken down, allowing the emergence of unexpected creativity, newness and hope. So being brought near to despair can be a great occasion and opportunity for the practice of faith. Indeed, it is most often in that place – if you can find the faith to stay there – that God helps us to find sufficient answer for a next step in a hopeful direction.

One of my favourite theologians, the cartoonist Mel Calman, has a splendid collection entitled *My God* – a figure portrayed as a little man in a nightshirt who inhabits a cloud. In one cartoon he is sitting on his cloud looking pained and the caption reads: 'I feel an Apocalypse coming on.' I find this picture very relevant to our times. Looking at our world and what we human beings are doing to it and ourselves, I sometimes find myself pretty close to despair. The pressures are so great and the folly seems so obvious. Perhaps there should be a notice placarded on our globe: 'wealth production is bad for your health'. Practically everyone knows this but hardly anyone is prepared to get organised to cope with it. We lack any wise insights into what is worth preserving, preventing and promoting for the future of our life together on a crowded and limited planet. We seem to be either euphorically drugged or complacently anaesthetised by a sort of collective, short-sighted stupidity. We bank on our inventiveness helping us out of one self-induced 'limited' situation after another while evidence piles up around us that we have gone beyond the stage of being able to keep ourselves on our chosen path by piecemeal solutions to individual pressures. Surely the ecological threats and the mass poverty and human misery we face in our One World today combine to make it clear that we must change our course and our priorities if we are to prevent humanity polluting itself out of existence or merely blowing itself up on the back of conflicting and absurd demands for various rigorous fundamentalisms.

It has been said of the Church of England that it is in favour of change as long as it does not make any difference. This is probably true of the British as a whole. Our political thinking tends to take its slogans from the past and is remarkably unready to adapt for a different future. This hesitancy applies, I think, to most fairly well-to-do people. We all want to preserve but we find the price of conservation – a change of habit and style of living – unreasonable, in our present terms, to the point of being unthinkable. So what are we to do? Is there really 'no alternative'?

One of the features of the prophetic message and insight as reinforced in Jesus is that apocalyptic pressures, if they are responded to by repentance and appropriate action, can be transmuted into the possibilities of hope. Can be, but may not be. This is part of our freedom and part of the space that God allows. As far as I can see, our faith in the God and Father of Our Lord Jesus Christ who offers to work with us in and through the Spirit, gives us absolutely no guarantee of earthly success on any front whatever. What our faith does offer is the assurance and certainty that there is no such thing as total failure. The situation, until the end, is always open – and open always to creative and redeeming possibilities. The challenge is to find the courage and vision for repentance in these, at times terrifying, pressures of reality.

Present reality includes the fact that the age of dogmatisms is over – though of course it is not yet done with. There is no infallible Church interpreted by a guaranteeing hierarchy. There is no infallible Book with guaranteed interpreters. There is no infallible science interpreted by guaranteeing experts. There is no infallible politics developed by a guaranteeing party, and still less is there an infallible State run by the right party. The critical question, the critical human, religious – and indeed political – question, is whether this discovery that all authorities are less authoritative than we thought should be treated as a paralysing disaster or as an exciting – however risky – set of opportunities.

The question is: how do we go on? I think we are in a betwixt and between stage where one sort of society has nearly run down and we are now having to learn how to be another sort of society. A real alternative might well have to be concerned with what, in theological language, are known as repentance and conversion – what might be translated in secular terms as thinking again and being changed accordingly.

What sort of clues does the faith I have sketched out in this book give us to the direction of the rethinking and relearning – the conversion – which will be required both in the Church and in secular politics and economics, if we are to find the hopeful future that I am clear God offers us? I believe there are signs as to where we should start.

To begin with the Church. We are not living in easy times; we face real dangers. It is important that Christianity is rescued from becoming a sect of religious sects among the competing and optional religious cults of the world. Faith can never be just for ourselves, for that is a contradiction of the universal message of Pentecost, and a contradiction of the Kingdom which is the power and worth and love of God for the whole of Creation. The temptation to take refuge in rigid and exclusive dogmatisms is great. However, although it is surprising what the Church can get wrong, I remain hopeful in the knowledge that even the Church cannot keep a good God down. We can, and must, avoid being sucked back into undesirable obsolescence, aping an authoritarian Church in a medieval society, or being trapped in the sociological naïveté that moral leadership is keeping the lower orders in their subordinate places.

For myself I do not have – and never have had – any fears for the future of Christianity. Indeed, a concern for its future seems to me to be wholly irrelevant. The faithful Christian part of me is fearless; for it is clear that the gates of hell cannot prevail against the true Church and the true Gospel of God. The merely 'human' part of me could not care less; if God cannot cope with secularisation and contemporaneity then he is no god and we should have none of him. One of the problems of Christianity in its more institutional forms is that it does tend not to have all that much to do with Jesus, but this need not depress us unduly. 'Semper reformanda' – having to re-learn and renew is a great and regular feature of the Tradition. Today, as in the past, the challenge to Christians is to face up to their Faith and from it to contribute to the new learning about lifestyles which is now plainly required.

In the Church of England we have to acknowledge that we are no longer in the Church of the Land in the old historical and all embracing sense. We have been put on a very awkward spot because we have, for instance, very few clues as yet to how we should reply to pressures such as those sketched out in the *Faith in the City* report and, more recently, the *Faith in the Countryside* document. But if past experience is to be believed, being on this awkward spot might turn out to be a highly promising and exciting spot if we can find the courage to stay on it and face its challenges together. We have a splendid chance to discover and demonstrate new ways of being the Church for the Land and to the Land – especially if we declare our faith and take fresh initiatives from our own resources in careful and determined relationship with fellow Christians in other denominations and churches in our neighbourhood.

However, if, in the Church of England, we go on simply concentrating on our recent divisions and preoccupations it will do grave damage. (The conflict over the Ordination of women is a prime example of such destructive preoccupations. Surely women must be ordained to the priesthood and we must use our internal resources to cope with that minority within the church who will be hurt by this.) It is urgent that we shift concentration from such side-issues to things that really matter to people in society at large – issues such as what is happening to our world, the business of loving our neighbours in real, down-to-earth situations. We need to face the fact that the real question is not the things that many church committees discuss, or church parties want to debate. The real question is: Can you really believe in a down-to-earth God as you proclaim in Jesus, in the work of the Spirit today, in the light of what we see going on around us and in the light of what we now know about the Bible?

Christians are in the business of helping people to discover that we are all on our way to the Kingdom of God where all relationships will be fulfilled. Christians should be contributing wherever they can to examples of sharing and enjoyment as signs of the greater sharing which is offered in the End. Now we only get glimpses; we only have the chance to offer glimpses to other people but the hope is that these glimpses will be fulfilled in the Kingdom of God. Sceptics may say that this is hardly enough to warrant conviction. It is up to Christians to so 'let their light shine' by the way they behave, and the communities they are part of, to demonstrate the truth of the glimpses they have of God as shown us by Jesus Christ. It is only by treating people, and each other, as created beings in the image of God and living by and through that belief that we can so let our light shine.

I begin to see a renewed and renewing Church in this land emerging, as it were, like a fresh and more beautiful butterfly out of the rather dull and dry chrysalis of the institution we seem to have fossilised into at the moment. I cannot see the shape of this newness at all clearly, yet I am sure that the Holy Spirit is around and ready to show us (if we will only let Him/Her) the way to grow into this new Church. But we must let go and grow.

According to the account in Genesis, Abraham was seventy-five years old when he was called to put his experience and his wisdom at God's disposal for the sake of the future. (It is clear that God takes no account of early retirement.) This involved literally moving out: 'And Abraham journeyed on, going by stages towards the Negeb'. He became a stranger and a pilgrim, but he was at home with God and his whole life was going somewhere until the very end of his life because he was a part of the purposes of God and knew that he was. He may not have had a detailed assurance of where he was going to end up, but there was nothing lost or unproductive about Abraham. We Christians need to remember Abraham and be ready to go out into our society, keeping it in mind that if God is to lead us out we must not act small within the confines of our own fears and pride but we must be inspired by dreams big beyond the confines of our own inadequacies.

Our doctrine of God needs to recapture the sense of mystery. Christian discipleship demands a moving on from the triumphalist view of godly power to the notion of a Creator Artist who has risked creating men and women in His image in the midst of the vastness of the universe – created beings infinitesimally small in scale but with an amazing capacity to love and to understand to an infinite degree. To believe in a God who is a Creator requires coming to terms with the notion that He did not create a perfect world. Only an understanding of God having set something – some project of Creation – in motion which requires collaboration between Him and women and men in order to work it out, makes any sense of this.

The Church in this context can be seen not primarily as an institution which needs in some impossible way to regain an authoritative voice in society, but as a community of communities. A community of communities who are set free by their faith in God, their worship of God, and their vision of what God is and offers in Jesus Christ, set free by all this to face the realities of our social and personal lives and to live and work, hopefully in the midst of them. Moral service is not a question of delivering heavenly revelations to be applied on a secularised earth. Heavenly revelations have no earthly use. It is a question of getting strength from the revelations so far received in order to so engage with the personal and social stuff of our daily lives that fresh revelation is received right here on the ground.

The churches have great work to do in building up communities of endurance around a celebration of the Gospel of the God who is committed to our world, our society and our future for the sake of His Kingdom. It is certain that there will be much to endure, including uncertainty, turbulence – even violence – and moments of feeling that there is no hope and no way forward. In God and under God this is not true. Christians can make a significant contribution to society, but only if they have the courage when put in a difficult position – or have a question to which they do not have the answer – to stay there in that Wilderness. For Christians know that our destiny lies with God and we know that if we stand, as a community, in a betwixt and between place, then a Christian may stand honestly in that betwixt and between place seeking to work out what it means to love God, love our neighbours and cherish the earth.

The era of Christendom is over. We Christians have to rediscover what it means to go out into the world and proclaim the Gospel. There are similarities in our present situation with the challenge which faced the Church in the third and fourth centuries. As then, we now have to work out in contemporary terms what are the implications of our belief that the ultimate reality lies in what we have learnt in Jesus, through the Spirit, about God. Christians need to escape from their own religious idolatry so that they can be set free to fight for the Kingdom against the idols of our society, those idols which are threatening to destroy our society by divisiveness and our world by pollution and exhaustion. They are age-old idols of riches, of self and of power for one's own sake. Old idols erected into unbridled pursuit of consumption, unrestrained competition and unfeeling individualism by specious dogmas about the way the world must be run, regardless of the costs to both community and the future.

Enough of the Church, what about the pressure of realities on politics and economics? What unthinkable questions are being pressed upon us?

Among other things, the pressures of present reality are calling in question the presuppositions on which politics and economics have been conducted for the last 200 years or more. These presuppositions rest on the assumption that the way to promote the maximum human happiness and well-being is by achieving the 'proper' organisation of production. We are now facing the fact of the disintegration of the dream of what growth, science, technology, combined with efficient production and distribution born in the Industrial Revolution, can achieve. It has led us to a system whereby growth in production has become equated with, and dependent on, growth in money-making. The only way of making money is by increasing production of goods and services for consumption by those who have the purpose and power. The evidence is emerging all around us of the side effects of this system. It is using up the earth, producing a terrible number of poor people, adding greatly to threatening pollution, while money – and therefore power – falls to a small number of quite unnecessarily rich and potentially irresponsible people or groups. All together we seem to have got caught up in a stupid, threatening and unsatisfying way of life which does not look like having much of a future, and one whose future does not, on the whole, seem very worthwhile even if we could reach it.

The ways and means of production have got to be drastically changed. We have got to face up to finding ways of there being much less of our most polluting and extravagant forms of production – and this logically involves less consumption of the sort practically everybody except the lowest consumers indulge in. This is far more revolutionary than anything Marx ever dreamt of. It seems clear that our survival demands that we rethink our priorities and reassess what we mean by costs, profits and wealth.

For instance, at present 'profit' appears to be regarded as the essential contribution which can and must be made to our future, but what about the cost of the way we pursue profits? It is now becoming increasingly apparent that the way 'we' (in particular enterprises) earn profits, and what 'we' (in the enterprise culture in general) count as profits, is costing us the possibility of a sustainable future. Budgets and balance sheets are focused on the profits obtained from the machinery, the materials, the processes and labour of the enterprise budgeted for. The sustaining and developing of a healthy workforce, or contributions to preserving the ecology of the planet, are not 'products' which at present add to the plus side of the balance sheet, but rather 'costs' which add to the debit side. It is something of a sick joke that so few find it odd in our society that we should put cash profit before human life and health and the health of the environment that sustains human life. We need to achieve a state where the profits which fuel the continuance of production are not earned at the cost of human life and environment.

Unless and until we can rethink and re-plan what we mean by wealth and what we count as wealth we shall be steadily discounting the future of our present prosperity and shall continue to increase the damage we are already inflicting on our personal and global health and chances for a healthy and prosperous future.

Which brings us to the need to develop a new politics. At the moment we do not have suitable structures. We have got to work out how the costs actually fall and we need to find a sufficient will to face and bear those costs. This requires new instruments for reaching participatory agreement and the means to implement such agreement. The present formal, legal and local institutions for planning and decision-taking do not seem to be working. We do not have enough trust, enough shared vision, enough participation. Together – ordinary citizens as much as professional politicians – we need to develop our politics to meet these new challenges.

A new politics would need to rethink critical questions such as: what makes a human being productive? Is a human being only productive when he or she is directly contributing to the means of increasing consumption? Or is a human being productive as long as he or she is making some contribution to the quality of life? In a consumer society where it looks as if what is called 'standards of living' could go on going up, we have been bamboozled into believing that people can only enjoy themselves, be enjoyable and share life with one another if they have a whole lot of material things as well. The belief that the only way to make money is to produce more and more goods and services for people to consume has created a wasteful society which encourages the production of a vast amount of often unnecessary things that are chucked away as soon as they are used; we are burying our chances beneath our piles of waste. I am not advocating some sort of puritan rejection of all material things. The question is about how we re-learn something which simpler societies have known for a long time and we seem to have forgotten – that is, that *people* are a society's best resources. Christians ought to be particularly good at helping one another and society at large to relearn this lesson.

The new society necessary to a sustainable future cannot be invented from scratch. It cannot be stumbled upon or cobbled together in five minutes or encapsulated in even the most brilliant political theory. It has to be worked out, step by step, struggled through and wrestled out on the ground by persons. There is much to learn and much to invent. We have to work out our understanding and practice for the next stage of our political and social search with an awareness that progress towards justice and social peace requires much sharper choices than we might like, and is under much more difficult conditions of wealth creation than we are accustomed to reckon with.

As guide and lodestone of the great search which is before us, there must be something kept alive in society which insists – even when it seems like hoping against hope – that men and women are never to be exhaustively defined or treated in the terms of any categorisation or ideology which claims to define reality for society and all human beings. The symptom of such a claim, which is at least threateningly incipient, is the tendency to remark that 'there is no alternative'.

If we are to avoid tyranny and what I would call the decadence of trivialising pseudo-absolutes (so much of both our arguing and our aims are currently dangerously trivialising), it is imperative that a sense of transcendent value and a commitment to human persons as being, at least potentially, far more than they seem to be at any one time, be kept practically alive by vision, by hope, by faith – and by sheer determined cussedness.

As a final thought under this heading of thinking unthinkable questions, I would like to suggest that a repentance (rethinking) around the worth of persons might well involve a rethinking of the whole business and concept of being an owner. It is perhaps an initially disturbing and scaring thought, but the Fathers of the Church taught that either ownership was to be related and exercised as stewardship, or it was theft. This is beginning to get a little near to the bone but perhaps we have to return to investigating such notions, if acquisitive and aggressive ownership is now counter-productive in a limited and socially stressed and divided world. Is it actually essential to human happiness for people to be dominated by the desire to possess, at any rate to possess more and more? Is it really too fanciful to wonder whether it might not be possible to persuade people to be content with having *sufficient* use, security, opportunity for adequate private expenditure and identity, so that we could all live more justly and peaceably?

I can imagine by now that the sceptics among us have had quite enough wishy-washy, liberal idealism. As a practising theologian I am adjusted to the difficulty – if not the impossibility – of my subjects. A theologian is always being asked to unscrew the inscrutable and should he succeed, however slightly, in showing that behind these difficult theological phrases there is something very human, very important and potentially divine, then the faithful will always tell him that he is not a believer and unbelievers will always tell him that he is asking them to believe too much. Yet still the central question remains: do we really have the resources, energy and vision to make a better world? Here, I believe, Christians ought to have some contribution to make, for we remain convinced that we actually do live as creatures not chances. This puts us in a position of great risk, but the risk is also opportunity. Our faith gives us conviction about resources of altruism, goodness and love which can again and again be made available or found to be available. It is amazing what men and women of commitment and vision and hope can do. I am personally convinced from the depths of my being that living together in community is what life is about and it is the most lively, lasting and enjoyable and continuing form of life, however precarious. At all costs we must not succumb to this notion of homo-economicus as an evolutionary deterministic individual who can be solely concerned with gaining what he or she can, so that there may be a sort of restricted charitable activity within a small family or similar unit. This is nonsense, trivialising of our humanity, and quite wrong.

Whatever the threats I continue to see signs of hope. The learning is beginning (as evidenced, partly, in the spin-offs and public awareness of the so-called 'Green awakening'). At times you may feel it will not happen fast enough, but as one tends to love oneself and other human beings, as life remains rather lovely and as one has hope in God, the expectation remains that something can be done. If you live at 11.59 there still lacks one whole minute to midnight and that minute might be long enough if we work at it. William Temple, among others, pointed out that the way to move towards righteousness in political matters is to bring people to realise the prudence of the arguments. Under the pressures of one world the visions of idealists are steadily moving from sentimentality to sheer facing of reality and the needs of survival. But working at the necessary rearrangement of priorities involves education, re-thinking and conversion at the level of institutions, professions and pressure groups.

Many people look at the world today and feel that humanity has lost its way. The problem, I believe, is not so much the existence of a widespread sense that our society lacks moral leadership, but the existence of widespread evidence that our society does not function as a society at all, at least in the sense of a society which is an effective community. There is a parallel to this with regard to the moral bewilderment and lostness of the individual. The real problem does not lie in the fact that there is no longer a clear authoritative voice which tells us what we should do and what we should believe. The real problem is that there seems to be no community which supports us and shares with us as we have to work out what we are to believe and what we are to do. Dogmatic institutions have broken down, and we do not live under authority as our ancestors did (or as we imagine they did), but we have not sufficiently developed the collaborative and supportive institutions which are appropriate for the current forms of human living, searching, hoping, enduring and enjoying. This is where we come to the practical crux, as I conceive it, about the Church and the moral leadership of contemporary society.

What is needed in the present state of our society are communities of people who face the facts and the issues of our contemporary life with realism, but also with hope – realism and hope sustained by vision and faith. Deepening realism is a very painful business, because to do this we must go beyond tribalism. What we and our group see is always limited and limiting. We need people with the courage to risk getting outside themselves and their own groups – tribes, classes, unions, professional organisations, churches, whatever. This really involves suffering. I think it is the modern equivalent of one version of going outside the camp with the Lord. (See Hebrews 13:12 following, 'Jesus also . . . suffered without the gate. Let us go forth therefore unto him without the camp "bearing his reproach".') But the suffering must be worthwhile because it is the only way to newness and hope.

It is quite clear that the present slogans and the present practices are getting nowhere fast. The one thing you can be absolutely sure about is that anybody who is absolutely sure about the answer to a problem is wrong. It follows from that that anyone who thinks he or she can deal with any matter adequately in two minutes on television is not worth listening to. There is a need to discover such a simplicity of faith that people will reject this simplicity about complexities. That is why we need faith. If you do not have faith then you have to keep on simplifying and that makes a hell of a mess. There are no overall answers to our great problems, but people of faith and hope – and indeed of love – can always find a step to take.

That hymn which seems to be sung so often, politically as

well as religiously – 'Sit down, O men of God, ye cannot do a thing', is simply not true. If we are to develop a way of life which encourages greater realism, the advancing beyond tribalism, and the taking of new steps then we need to get organised. It should be a routine part of the life of every congregation (I use the phrase whether it means a congregation as a coming together of people in a church, or the coming together of people, a union or a professional group or whatever) in getting to grips with some problems and facing the facts.

A few years back there was a splendid Christmas card doing the rounds. On the front it had a cherubic choirboy, flushed in the face and stamping his foot. The caption read: 'Oh come *on*, all ye faithful!' It was a very good Christmas message for our times. Religiously the churches and their members have to look for grace from the God in whom they say they believe, to free them from immoral hankerings after false forms of authority, and above all from any illusions about infallibility. Collectively, we all as citizens, whether Christians or not, have to look for any help which we believe to be available to free us from the various forms of a widespread contemporary and secular illusion. This is that there is some right form of combining something from science and something from politics, which is bound, through a State run by the right people, progressively to promote material well-being, social justice, and human happiness. There are no infallible answers in this, or in any other human and vital area, and it may be quite wrong to go around looking and longing for moral leadership on the grounds that authority has broken down.

Faith does not provide answers; it obliges us to face the facts. If we will do this, God will give us a sufficient answer – which is often in fact about more realism, going beyond tribalism and taking the next step. The central truth of the human condition is that we must live with risk and the impossibility of the notion of 'getting it right' in any absolute, or eternal way. It is in the wrestling with risk and our own inadequacies, in the gulf between the reality of our falling short and the enticement of our dreams, that we reach beyond ourselves, borrowing from the edges of the transcendent power and glimpse wisdom. There is no such thing as 'getting it right' – or rather there are infinite ways of 'getting it right' – none of them absolute, or universal but infinitely personal.

St Paul has a phrase he used in his letter to the Colossians (1:27) 'Christ in you, the hope of glory'. Men and women are in God's image. We resonate to knowledge, to love, to longing and to glory. The worth which we glimpse in human faces, which we experience in ourselves, which we glimpse in the world and which we enjoy, above all, when we are simply loving or in love, is a real, open and powerful response to the God who is behind all, in all, through all and beyond all – and who wishes to share the worship of His love with us. We are 'in the image of God', at least as potential and promise, in a way which can and ought to make a difference to the way in which we live through, respond to and suffer from the sheer realities which we encounter. We are creatures not chances. So what about the possibility of Christ in you, the hope of glory? The chance of contributing to creativity, the chance of sharing in life, the chance of a deep and lasting enjoyment of heights and depths, of sheer livingness. Life might after all be about living and not about consuming or exploiting. If we will but stop and dare to attend and go into ourselves, we may indeed find there Christ in you, the hope of glory.

As it says in Paul's letter to the Philippians (4:4–8)

'Rejoice in the Lord always, and again I say rejoice [for there is life and love and possibility around, whether you are up or down]. Be careful for nothing, but in everything with prayer and supplication make your thanksgiving be known unto God and let your moderation be known unto all men.

Finally brethren, whatsoever things are true, whatsoever things are honest, whatsoever things are just, whatsoever things are pure, think on these things.'

People often fancy it is cool to be cynical and indifferent. The fact remains that it is honesty, a search for truth, a search for purity, a search for justice, an awareness of loveliness and an awareness of the possibility of things which will see us through any crisis.

In these times we live in we are plainly facing the spread of fundamentalisms, simplified ideologies and the peddling of solutions to problems at both the world level and for the individual which can be expressed in slogans and slick, instant moralisms. The current controversies about faith, authority and meaning going on in Christian churches are mirrored in Judaism and Islam. In secular politics we are seeing the degeneration of debate, compromise and consensus in favour of the adoption of dogmatic theories. Humanity is being threatened on both the religious and secular fronts by the effects of infantile simplicity and the old, cruel demons of dogma. Reaction to the discovery that neither the Enlightenment nor science and technology have turned out to be as promising as was supposed, and that, indeed, they have led to the production of many threatening things, is leading to a variety of recommendations that we should return to the attitudes and methods of the Dark Ages. We are facing a crisis within the whole Western intellectual and cultural tradition. It becomes ever more vital that worship of the One True Living God be reinstated as a crucial resource in exposing and challenging the false and destructive limitations of all philosophies, theories, and religious interpretations raised to the status of dogmas.

Religious faith must not be allowed only to survive as the highly sectarian and individualistic 'spiritual' back-up for groups like those which coalesce into the 'Moral Majority', or be the spiritual glue for the lives of ethnic and cultural minorities who need this faith to preserve their own ghettos and identities. The Gospel needs to be preached. It needs to be preached now and it needs to be preached in such ways that people have some chance of picking up the message. Thousands of people today are getting nothing but messages of worthlessness and hopelessness. This is blasphemous and contrary to the love and good news of God. So much in our society and in our own behaviour is simply idolatrous and destructively self-centred. We must receive the Grace of God to free ourselves from idols and to witness against the idols of society. For all the attempts from many quarters to marginalise God as merely a 'religious' question, the pressures of the reality we now face are reinstating what might shortly but inadequately be called 'the God question' as the central question at the heart of living matters to do with civilisation, culture and society.

Index